A BIBLIOGRAPHY OF

NEGRO
HISTORY
&
CULTURE

FOR YOUNG READERS

MILES M. JACKSON, JR.

COMPILER AND EDITOR

ASSISTED BY

MARY W. CLEAVES

AND

ALMA L. GRAY

PUBLISHED FOR ATLANTA UNIVERSITY
BY THE UNIVERSITY OF PITTSBURGH PRESS

A BIBLIOGRAPHY OF

NEGRO

HISTORY

CULTURE

FOR YOUNG READERS

"As I Grew Older" quoted by permission from *The Dream Keeper and Other Poems.* Copyright ©, 1932, Alfred A. Knopf, Inc. Renewed 1960 by Langston Hughes.

"Incident" from *On These I Stand* by Countee Cullen. Copyright ©, 1925, by Harper & Brothers; renewed 1953 by Ida M. Cullen. Reprinted by permission of Harper & Row, Publishers.

"We Shall Overcome" used by permission. New Words and Music Arrangement by Zilphia Horton, Frank Hamilton, Guy Carawan, and Pete Seeger. TRO © Copyright 1960 and 1963 Ludlow Music, Inc., New York, New York. Royalties derived from this composition are being contributed to The Martin Luther King, Jr., Fund.

CONTENTS

•

ACKNOWLEDGEMENTS

•

The Institute on Materials by and about Negro Americans, sponsored by Atlanta University in October 1965, recommended that a committee be established immediately to implement the recommendations that grew out of the institute. The people who served on that volunteer committee were Mrs. Mary W. Cleaves, Librarian, Sun Valley Junior High School, Los Angeles School District, California; Mrs. Alma L. Gray, Librarian, Douglass High School, Baltimore, Maryland; Miles M. Jackson, Jr., Librarian, Atlanta University, Atlanta, Georgia; Dr. Virginia L. Jones, Dean, School of Library Service, Atlanta University, Atlanta, Georgia; Miss Mollie Lee, Librarian, Richard B. Harrison Public Library, Raleigh, North Carolina; H. Gilbert Nichol, Associate Director of Development, Princeton University, Princeton, New Jersey; Dr. Annette H. Phinazee, Head of Special Services, Atlanta University, Atlanta, Georgia; Mrs. Dorothy Porter, Supervisor, Moorland Foundation, Howard University, Washington, D. C.; M. D. Sprague (deceased), Librarian, Tuskegee Institute, Tuskegee, Alabama.

FOREWORD

"AND THE WALLS COME TUMBLING DOWN"

●

Childhood has been described, very frequently, as "the impressionable years." This is the period when certain events or situations which occur may remain vivid memories throughout the life span of an individual. Such childhood memories may be pleasant or they may have negative connotations, depending upon the circumstances which provided the means for unforgettable experiences.

Perhaps, one of the most impressionable happenings ever related is found in the poignant story poem, "Incident," by the brilliant young poet, Countee Cullen:

> Once riding in old Baltimore
> Heart-filled, head-filled with glee,
> I saw a Baltimorean
> Keep looking straight at me.

> Now I was eight and very small,
> And he was no whit bigger,
> And so I smiled, but he poked out
> His tongue, and called me, "Nigger."

> I saw the whole of Baltimore
> From May until December;
> Of all the things that happened there
> That's all that I remember.[1]

In this brief glimpse into the impressionable years of childhood, Countee Cullen shares a harsh reality learned at an early age. He reveals a children's world structured with a maze of dichotomous patterns. It contains a *social order,* polarized into black and white segments. It sustains an *emotional climate,* charged with elements of acceptance or rejection, love or hatred, trust or fear. It establishes *boundaries,* crowded with imprisoned people peering from behind invisible walls or impenetrable barriers.

For the white child in the poem, these invisible walls are transparent. Negatively, they resemble the "Looking-glass room" of the immortal Alice in Wonderland who exclaimed when she went "through the glass, and had jumped lightly down into the Looking-glass room. . . . 'Oh, what fun it'll be, when they see me through the glass in here, and can't get at me.' " Harmfully, such walls encase these children in a sterile environment where their growth is stunted and their sensibilities are dulled.

For the young Negro child in the poem, these invisible walls are impenetrable barriers. They loom dark and forbidding, expressing in their very presence a sense of exclusion. Corrosively, these walls destroy within these children the cherished dream alluded to by Langston Hughes in his poem "As I Grew Older."

> It was a long time ago.
> I have almost forgotten my dream.
> But it was there then,
> In front of me,
> Bright like the sun—
> My dream.
>
> And then the wall rose,
> Rose slowly,

---

[1] *On These I Stand,* New York: Harper & Row, 1947, p. 9.

Slowly,
Between me and my dream.
Rose slowly, slowly,
Dimming,
Hiding,
The light of my dream.
Rose until it touched the sky—
The wall.

Shadow.
I am black.

I lie down in the shadow.
No longer the light of my dream before me,
Above me.
Only the thick wall.
Only the shadow.

My hands!
My dark hands!
Break through the wall!
Find my dream!
Help me to shatter this darkness,
To smash this night,
To break this shadow
Into a thousand lights of sun,
Into a thousand whirling dreams
Of sun![2]

Within their microcosm of a larger-based world, children are already trapped. Victims of a practiced intolerant tolerance, children are confronted with confusing values of an adult-oriented society. We "prattle" to them about democratic principles; children view or join their counterparts living in "Resurrection Cities" or marching across the country "in protest" for the extension of democratic practices. We erect "show-case plazas" and high-income centers of urban renewal; children

---

[2] *The Dream Keeper and Other Poems,* New York: Alfred A. Knopf, 1932, pp. 74–75.

watch desperate segments of society, including girls and boys like themselves, indulge in self-inflicted property destruction as a last despairing cry to their unheeded voices. We extol the brave sacrifices of our youth on distant battle fields; children see (via telestar and satellite) their peers in strife-torn countries, numbered among the victims, growing up in abject hopelessness or dying by the thousands from starvation. We build our "invisible-walled," escapist suburbia; children don their "rose-colored" glasses to live in a "fool's paradise," insensitive to the intellectual and economic plight of their ghetto-bound counterparts who cannot escape.

In this world of dichotomous patterns, it is impossible for children to understand the significance of the words of Dr. Martin Luther King, Jr., in his famous speech, "I Have A Dream":

> I have a dream that my four little children will one day live in a nation where they will not be judged by the color of their skin but by the content of their character.[3]

Is it beyond reason for children to appreciate the implications of one of the recommendations for a pursuit of strategy as outlined in the *Report of the National Advisory Commission on Civil Disorders:*

> We have seen . . . the consequences of racial isolation, at all levels, and of attitudes toward race, on both sides, produced by three centuries of myth, ignorance and bias. It is indispensable that opportunities for interaction between the races be expanded. "The problems of this society will not be solved unless and until our children are brought into a common encounter and encouraged to forge a new and more viable design of life."[4]

Whether children sense the humane concern of a Dr. King

---

[3] Dorothy Sterling, *Tear Down the Walls! A History of the American Civil Rights Movement,* New York: Doubleday, 1968, p. 206.

[4] *Report of the National Advisory Commission on Civil Disorders,* New York: Bantam Books, 1968, p. 438.

or the urgency of meeting a crisis as envisioned by a national commission, one thing is certain. Children of all ethnic and religious groups (particularly, the black and the white) are affected, in varying degrees, by the stark reality of racism which engulfs them. There are still too many, today, who can play the role of the unfriendly white child or the trusting Negro lad in Countee Cullen's poem "Incident." Watching children struggling to extricate themselves from such towering walls of prejudice, a parent, a teacher, or a librarian must guide them with primary and secondary means and resources. Among the latter, one must include the media of communication. Again, in the words of the Presidential Commission on Civil Disorders:

> The major goal is the creation of a true union—a single society and a single American identity. Toward that goal, we propose . . . for national action:
>
> . . . .
>
> Increasing communication across racial lines to destroy stereotypes, to halt polarization, end distrust and hostility, and create common ground for efforts toward public order and social justice.[5]

While the adult carefully structures such a magnificent sounding goal and engages in speculative debate concerning methodology, children are already on the move. Time does not stand still for them. They do not wait for possible methods of communication to be explored or needless surveys and feasibility studies to be undertaken. Let the adult struggle with ways to communicate behind self-imposed walls of segregation and separation. Let the adult try to balance, fruitlessly, a need for communication with their denial to children to have rightful face-to-face confrontations with their ethnic counterparts in natural, childlike situations. Children have already discovered other avenues of escape from these isolated, unrealistic environments. They have achieved the desired communication.

Ironically, children have turned upon this scheming, inven-

[5] *Ibid.*, p. 23.

tive adult who seeks to keep them prisoners. Young people have used the very tools of their oppressors to open the gates to intellectual and, eventually, physical freedom. Pointedly, children declare, "Physically, you have made us your prisoners. We cannot associate with other girls and boys who are different from us. We cannot go to school with other girls and boys whose skin color is different from ours. We cannot share our lunches with other girls and boys who are kept apart from us. But, do not be too smug in your feelings of success. We will know who they are, where they live, and what they do. For you have given to us the means to discover these things through your most sophisticated forms of communication.

"In your age of enlightenment, you grant us limitless worlds to explore in vast libraries of literature. In your technological advances, you provide us with new vistas through the radio, the television, the film, and telestar. In your halls of learning, you teach us the fundamentals of reading; you instruct us in the techniques of machine operation. You give us these means to liberate our minds and to feed our impoverished spirits with a new sense of human understanding. Keep your physical walls; yet, they, too, in time, will come 'tumbling down.' "

As this chorus of predominantly white children, living behind their glass walls of prejudice, rises in crescendo, it is joined by equally vibrant voices of mostly Negro youth, excluded and "outside," who sing exultantly:

> We shall overcome, we shall overcome,
> We shall overcome some day.
> Oh, deep in my heart I do believe
> We shall overcome some day.
>
> We'll walk hand in hand, we'll walk hand in hand,
> We'll walk hand in hand some day,
> Oh, deep in my heart I do believe
> We shall overcome some day.
>
> The truth will make us free, the truth will make us free,
> The truth will make us free some day.

> Oh, deep in my heart I do believe
> We shall overcome some day.
>
> We shall live in peace, we shall live in peace,
> We shall live in peace some day,
> Oh, deep in my heart I do believe
> We shall overcome some day.[6]

Caught between these gradually combined choruses of determined youth, the bewildered adults are witnessing their cherished bulwarks, built upon a foundation of tenuous racism, slowly crumbling before the surging force of communication tools—books and multi-media instruments. In fearful dismay they watch television programs focused, as never before, upon the question of black–white relationships, black power, the ghetto, the negative effects of discrimination and segregation. They hear debates enlivened by racially-mixed panels, news reported by black and white analysts. They see Negro guests interviewed and entertainment programs sprinkled with more and more black artists. The adult is disturbed and begins to wonder at this black renaissance. And, as he looks, his children look. They, too, wonder, but not with fear, only with curiosity.

Watching their children and young people coming into their homes with borrowed library books, adults are "shaken," further, by some of the "new" reading enjoyed by their offspring: *Durango Street, The Empty Schoolhouse, Tituba of Salem Village, Jim Beckwourth: Negro Mountain Man, A Raisin in the Sun, Tear Down the Walls: A History of the American Civil Rights Movement.* Timidly, many adults are asking their children and young people, "Where is good old *Little Black Sambo?* What has happened to *Epaminondas* or *The Pickaninny Twins?* Couldn't you find *Uncle Remus* or *Gone With the Wind?* Why can't you be satisfied with *Up From Slavery* and that 'nice' story about Dr. George Washington Carver?"

---

[6] "We Shall Overcome," New York: Ludlow Music, 1960.

Politely listening but "tuning out" these queries, children and young people continue to establish contacts which transcend the invisible walls of prejudice through the multi-media outlets of communication and through the literary output of concerned writers. Turning their backs upon some of the "endearing" programs and literature of the past, these emerging socially conscious young individuals of a new generation are seeking answers to disturbing questions which trouble them. In their search for social values they read and ask: What is an "inner-city"? Who created this *Dark Ghetto: Dilemma of Social Power*? Is it true some of *Our Children Are Dying*? If so, to whom does this refer? Why hasn't *The Story of the Negro* been told before? Am I always going to be, prematurely, *A Manchild in the Promised Land*? What is the true cost of living in *A Glass House of Prejudice*? Why do people like me *But Not Next Door*? Will the entrance into our suburbs always have *The Barred Road*? How much difference is there in black–white living in *South Town* or *North Town*? What are the real issues behind the *Negro Revolution in America*? What adult practices have created *A Crisis in Black and White*? When will white America realize that it is *Time to Speak* on social issues? Can we enjoy, together, the fun of sharing *City Rhythms* and playing outside during *The Snowy Day*?

In their search for personal values, the younger generation reads and asks of its elders: Why am I considered *The Troublesome Presence*? Will you understand why I am compelled to *Stride Toward Freedom*? Where can I find the *Strength to Love* under such adverse conditions? Is it wrong if *I Always Wanted to be Somebody*? May I look to you for guidance and encouragement, for *I Have a Dream* to cherish? Will you have confidence in my abilities to be *The Contender* who will try to make you proud? Can you, who are older, understand our reasons *Why We Can't Wait* any longer? Will you trust our motives when we become *Classmates by Request*? How shall you show us for what ends we shall live as we walk *The Lonesome Road*?

From such questions, framed from the titles of a new body of literature they are reading, children and young people are establishing immediate lines of communication. Within the minds of some there is slowly evolving an awareness of others beyond their respective environmental walls of separation. In many instances, curiosity is giving way to a questioning concern. How much these young readers care, however, will depend upon their own degree of sensitivity which they bring to the new ideas found on the printed pages. Will this sensitivity enable them to project themselves into the lines, between the lines, and beyond the lines of print which captures their attention? One can only hope that such a concept of social sensitivity will emerge into reality. If this is possible, then, in the thinking of Louise Rosenblatt, from her book, *Literature as Exploration:*

> Prolonged contact with literature may result in increased social sensitivity. Through poems and stories and plays, the child becomes aware of the complex personalities of other people. He develops a stronger tendency to notice the reactions of others to his own behavior. He learns imaginatively to put himself into the place of the other fellow. He becomes better able to foresee the possible repercussions of his own actions in the life of others. In his daily relations with other people such sensitivity is precious.[7]

Yet, while some children and young people in the black–white communities will establish some lines of communication through the use of literature, others will be unaffected. For many "sheltered" white youth, the growing body of books by and about the Negro will remain "off-limits" in too many homes, schools, and libraries. A lack of black residents or "special racial problems" in many geographical areas may impel insensitive adults to conclude that such materials will have little or no local relevance for their "insulated" communities. Thus, school curricula, library collections, and home reading will remain im-

---

[7] *Literature as Exploration,* New York: Appleton-Century-Crofts, 1938, pp. 217–18.

poverished and incomplete. Communication will continue to be static and one-dimensional in nature.

Among the "excluded" black youth who are unaware of the upward surge of books by and about the Negro, such new entries into the broader sphere of the literature of mankind may remain totally unnoticed. Frequently victims of inferior educational programs of reading guidance, and denied adequate public, school, or home library facilities and collections, these young people will lack a proper motivation for turning to such books. So, they may continue to believe, with their limited knowledge of literature, that the only offerings available in this current period of unrest are still the fictitious stereotypes upon which they have been fed for generations.

Faced with these challenging issues, concerned librarians and educators are confronted with the formidable task of bringing together all segments of these young readers from every ethnic, racial, and social background and this exciting, enriching body of literature by and about the Negro. If one must have a mandate for this task, the need is found in an excerpt from the 1853 *Proceedings of the Colored National Convention* as recorded by Dorothy Sterling in her book, *Tear Down the Walls: A History of the American Civil Rights Movement:*

> Our white fellow countrymen do not know us. They are strangers to our character, ignorant of our capacity, oblivious of our history and progress, and misinformed as to the principles that guide us.[8]

The urgency for action is highlighted for us by Dr. James E. Allen, Jr., New York State Education Commissioner, who stated in his special message to school superintendents as reported in the New York *Times,* April 25, 1968:

> The obligations of schools to present history fully and accurately and to deal with current situations with faithfulness in fact and spirit, not only for minority group children, but for all children, is, of course, undeniable.

---

[8] *Op. cit.,* p. 44.

The demand for prompt attention to this educational objective is strong, and properly so, and the responsibility for action rests with all of us. To do otherwise will perpetuate a sense of inferiority and alienation for many and will continue to nurture the hostility and unreality born of ignorance and misinformation.[9]

The call for the implementation of the stated need is contained in the *Report of the National Advisory Commission on Civil Disorders* which suggests the adoption of the following educational practice to improve school performance:

Recognition of the history, culture and contribution of minority groups to American civilization in the textbooks and curricula of all schools. In addition, school curricula should be adapted to take advantage of student experiences and interest in order to stimulate motivation.[10]

Already aware of these challenging views, a committee of concerned librarians meeting at Atlanta University, Atlanta, Georgia, in 1965, began to work on a project called "A buying guide for materials by and about Negro Americans to be used primarily by librarians serving children and youth." The result of this effort is this compilation, *A Bibliography of Negro History and Culture for Young Readers*. Its purposes are in keeping with the stated goal of the National Commission on Civil Disorders to establish "a true union—a single society and a single American identity." Further, the list provides another means for "increasing communication across racial lines to . . . create common ground for efforts toward public order and social justice." Specifically, the objectives are as follows:

1. Provide teachers and librarians with a buying list which will help them in developing more well-rounded book collections.

---

[9] P. 35.
[10] *Op. cit.,* p. 447.

2. Provide opportunities for pupils to observe the inter-relationship of people within our nation.
3. Provide realistic and practical applications for pupils to evaluate contributions of Negroes in relationship to other Americans.
4. Provide sound background as well as current materials and, therefore, ensure better understanding and learning experiences.

If librarians and educators are to make the most effective use of this bibliography, it is imperative for each one to be responsive to both the intended audience for whom the selections were made and to the material itself. It will be a new experience for some to establish an empathic relationship with a young individual or a group who may not have been included in one's "exclusive" environment. How well such an adjustment is made will depend upon the ability of the adult to alter, modify, or relinquish preconceived stereotyped attitudes and beliefs. How much understanding is brought by the adult to guide children and young people to develop an appreciation of each other's similarities and differences depends upon the degree of sensitivity sustained within the educator and the librarian.

Equally important in using this prepared material is one's knowledge of the contents of each of the entries. Nothing is more damaging to reading guidance than this all-too-frequent lack in adults. Young readers are quickly responsive to insincerity. Unerringly, they will expose the adult's masquerade of pretentious book knowledge with two simple questions: "Did you read it? What's it about?" They will spurn the offered book if its intent is to serve merely a utilitarian purpose rather than to meet an immediate interest or need.

Children will not read the titles on the list willingly if they are to be "developed" or instructed. However, they will be pleased to read the entries if the educator or librarian can challenge them with the ideas and the provocative thoughts the books contain. Thus the task in using this compilation is placed in its proper perspective. Help young readers to find in these selections new, different roads to travel. Open doors into the many faceted worlds of the Negro. Help young people to relate to the individual and to situations which they encounter in these worlds with a humane understanding. Our youthful readers have the capacity for this universal characteristic.

This is a belief so beautifully expressed in a personal Christmas greeting received from Elizabeth B. deTrevino, author of and Newbery Award recipient for her distinguished novel, *I, Juan de Pareja,* a story based upon the life of the Negro slave of the famous Spanish artist Velasquez:

> In one special quality common to all children, we may have the foundation stone on which we can construct a lasting peace. It has been there to . . . hand down through the centuries; each generation of children, the world over, puts it into our hands anew. . . . I refer to the capacity for empathy. Children can identify with all things and all creatures. Brotherhood is natural to them. If, then, we foster and preserve and mature this empathy, the men and women they become will be able to know the people of the earth by sharing their being. Then, I think, we can build; we can really achieve that ultimate good, "peace on earth."

If librarians and educators accept this premise and assume the commitments it implies, then this bibliography will serve as another link in the communication network so essential to help destroy the invisible walls created to separate the worlds of white and Negro children.

SPENCER G. SHAW
Consultant, Library Service to Children
Nassau Library System
Garden City, New York

INTRODUCTION

In October 1965 an Institute on Materials by and about Negro Americans was sponsored by the School of Library Service of Atlanta University. Appropriately, the institute was held simultaneously with the fiftieth conference of the Association for the Study of Negro Life and History. The purposes of the institute were to provide an opportunity to review the present status of library materials by and about Negro Americans and to delineate areas of future growth and expansion; to consider specific methods of increasing access to these materials; and to establish or strengthen communications among librarians and scholars so that library materials can be acquired and used more efficiently.

During the three days of meetings on the campus of Atlanta University, the participants in the institute discussed the varied problems of supplying students, teachers, and scholars with the information necessary for study of the Negro's contribution to America. The institute particularly recognized a pressing need for a critical guide to books and other materials appropriate for young readers.

Despite the efforts of local governments, the federal government, and many citizens' organizations, Negroes have not yet been fully integrated into the mainstream of American life and culture. Although it has been over three hundred years since the first Africans landed on the shores of this continent, their contribution to American life has remained unrecognized. From the very beginning, black men have been an integral part of the struggles to build this great nation: they tilled the soil of the great Southern plantations from sunup to sundown; they helped to lay the railway tracks that crossed the continent; and they fought in all the wars, from the Revolutionary War to the present conflict in Vietnam. Negro Americans have contributed to the arts, education, science, government, politics, and sports. Unfortunately, most Americans are unaware of the Negro's record of accomplishment; in fact, many young Negroes themselves are oblivious to the contributions of other Negroes to the growth and development of this country. The fault can be placed in many areas: local government, schools and their governing bodies, curriculum planning, teaching, churches, and even the home.

Since the strengths and weaknesses of this country rest mainly on the extent and thoroughness of its educational system, it is through education that this gross oversight can be remedied. As early as 1891, Edward A. Johnson, teacher and historian, commented:

> I have often observed the sin of omission and commission on the part of white authors, most of whom seem to have written exclusively for white children, and studiously left out the many creditable deeds of the Negro. The general tone of most of the histories taught in our schools has been that of inferiority of the Negro.[1]

For too long Negroes have been left out of American history and social studies in our schools. In some cases this oversight has been intentional, while in others it is the result of neglect. In those instances when Negroes have been included in textbooks, they have often been the objects of ridicule or have

[1] *A School History of the Negro Race in America*, New York: Goldman Co., 1911, p. 3.

been depicted as not having contributed at all to the American heritage. Dr. Charles Wesley, a noted historian, has stated:

> History, read and taught, in the schools, should not be the story of people of one color with the neglect and omission of the men and women of another race or color. When a part of the people, a minority as a group, has been neglected or given subordinate place, history for a truthful presentation should be reconstructed and not neglected, in the interest of good human relations.[2]

In recent years there has been some attempt to include facts about Negroes in history and social studies texts, but much more has been accomplished outside of textbook publishing. Numerous small school districts, however, are unable to provide the bibliographic tools and review media necessary to keep up with the many books on Negroes that are now being published. Some large school districts have at various times prepared bibliographies on Negroes, but these bibliographies are usually distributed only within the preparing district. Also, they are usually incomplete or otherwise limited in scope, they are without sufficient information about the included titles to facilitate careful selection, and, in most instances, they are without information about audiovisual materials. Then, too, many small school districts lack trained library personnel, and few librarians and teachers in districts of all sizes have the specialized knowledge necessary to make a good selection in such a potentially sensitive area.

Bibliographic materials of titles by and about Negro Americans have been available. An early one, Monroe Work's *Bibliography of the Negro in Africa and America,* was first published in 1928. This exhaustive guide contains more than 17,000 titles of books, pamphlets, and periodical articles, and includes writings in English, German, French, Spanish, Italian, Portuguese, and other languages. Although Work's bibliography is

---

[2] *Neglected History: Essays in Negro American History,* Wilberforce, Ohio: Central State College Press, 1965, p. 25.

considered basic to any scholarly research on Negroes, it is inappropriate for the librarian serving young readers because of its date and its scholarly approach. The National Urban League published a *Selected Bibliography of the Negro* in 1940 and has issued supplements periodically. This listing, while it is commendable, is dated and was not planned specifically for young readers. Edgar and Alma Thompson's *Race and Region: A Descriptive Bibliography* (1949) is a comprehensive classified bibliography limited to race relations. The basis of its compilation is to bring together special references to relations between whites and Negroes in the United States. More recent publications are *The Negro in the United States* (1965) by Erwin K. Welsch, and *The Negro in America: A Bibliography* (1966) by Elizabeth Miller. Welsch's work is considered a research guide and is written in the form of a bibliographic essay. Originally a mimeographed guide prepared for students and librarians at Indiana University, it was not planned for elementary and high school students. Miller's compilation originated as part of an extensive study of Negroes in the United States conducted by the American Academy of Arts and Sciences, and was published in two parts by *Daedalus*. It is a scholarly work and is comprehensive; there is no attempt at selectivity.

Perhaps the most nearly ideal guide to books on Negroes for young readers is Augusta Baker's *Books about Negro Life for Children* (1963). This valuable listing is published by the New York Public Library. However, Miss Baker's work is limited in scope and does not include audiovisual materials. Charlemae Rollins compiled for the National Council of Teachers of English a selected list entitled *We Build Together* (1967), which covers material for preschool through ninth grade readers. Erwin A. Salk's *A Layman's Guide to Negro History* (1966), "intended to show the depth of the Negro's contribution to the history of our country," includes a very brief section on books for children.

Thus, by and large the materials teachers need to help them introduce young readers to information on Negroes in America are limited, a situation this bibliography attempts to remedy.

It is an annotated list of books and audiovisual materials recommended for teaching the role of Negroes in the development of American life, as well as Negro heritage and traditions. The notes that are included with each entry indicate the unique features that will appeal to specific curricula interests. The selection guide will be of particular value to small school districts in recommending materials for factual information on the Negro American. This is not to say that the large school districts will not find the *Bibliography* of value in planning units in history and social sciences. Even the large school districts have been limited in their inclusion of materials pertinent to the study of Negro Americans, despite the lists published by school districts in Baltimore, Chicago, and Los Angeles.

The *Bibliography* will provide teachers, librarians, and parents with a list of materials that will make possible logical steps in planning instruction on the Negro American for both classroom and home. Specifically, the work is intended to provide teachers and librarians with a buying list that will help them to develop more well-rounded book collections. The *Bibliography* will also provide opportunities for pupils to observe the interrelationships of people within our nation and will demonstrate to them realistic and practical applications for evaluating contributions of Negroes in relation to those of other Americans. The need of a comprehensive tool such as this bibliography is imperative in light of the slow changes in textbook treatment of Negroes, the increasing quantity and quality of materials being produced on the subject, and the demand, currently expressed by students, teachers, and parents, for information on Negro Americans.

Mass migrations from rural sections to urban ones since the close of World War II, plus improved communications and trends in economics and social relations, have made all Americans next-door neighbors. Many students feel the need of a deeper grasp of Negro–white relationships, and find in books the logical place to satisfy this need. Teachers are challenged to focus attention on the biased treatment of Negroes in school curricula. It is hoped that in the very near future a child will not be given "books to read and study, films to observe, concepts . . . to be understood and learned, in which all necessary, heroic and functioning people are white, with not even a suggestion that this view of our society is totally unrealistic."[3] All is not lost, and the hopeful note is the continued and sustained work of Negro and white scholars, as few as they are, who see the importance of recording the place of Negroes in the annals of history.

MMJ

---

[3] Lerone Bennett, Jr., "Reading, 'Riting, and Racism," *Ebony,* March, 1967, p. 130.

NATURE AND USE
OF THE BIBLIOGRAPHY

Three librarians with extensive experience in the field of Negro American literature compiled the *Bibliography* through the use of standard bibliographic tools, published by acknowledged book selection agencies and organizations. In addition, such sources as book lists distributed by private and governmental human relations groups and current periodicals aimed at young readers were thoroughly examined. The compilers also used various recently published monographs on Negroes, including the bibliographies compiled at Indiana University and Harvard University, and edited these lists to provide maximum usefulness for the intended audience.

That audience covers a wide age range, from Pre-school through Senior High School. The scope of the *Bibliography* includes all fields of literature: Fiction, the Social Sciences, Pure and Applied Sciences, Arts, Drama, Poetry, Essays, History, and Biography. Concerning the latter field, each biography has been placed under the subject that comes closest to the work or specific interest of the biographee. Thus, Sammy Davis, Jr.'s *Yes, I Can* is found under the subject category, ARTS. (A separate list of the biographies included in this *Bibliography* is provided in Appendix I.) Special attention has been focused upon multi-media materials: films, recordings, pictures, and other non-book aids.

The entries have been carefully evaluated and selected in accordance with established criteria used in "screening" any recommended book or non-book material. The selections have also been considered in terms of their social significance and their integrity in presenting, positively, the Negro as a subject or as a creative writer. Books for Senior High readers will include many works drawn from the field of literature for adults. These have been selected because of their timeliness, their honesty in presenting provocative ideas and factual information, and their appeal to young people who have the intellectual and emotional maturity to appreciate the contributions of these creative works in helping them gain a broader perspective of issues and challenges in this important age of social change.

Each entry contains complete bibliographical information: author, title, publisher, copyright date, and price. (Prices given are retail, unless only library price is available.) Brief annotations describe the contents of the book. In some descriptive notes, suggested ways to use the book are given. Recognizing the limitations of some users in determining grade or age levels of the books, the compilers devised a suggested set of guidelines:

1. The entries have been divided into two major Divisions: ELEMENTARY and SECONDARY.
2. Within these Divisions, suggested subdivisions have been created. These are merely guides and are not intended to be inflexible. Each librarian and educator will use individual judgment to determine which titles are most suitable for slow, average, or accelerated readers.

ELEMENTARY DIVISION
(Books for Children)

Coding

LE	Lower Elementary
LE-I	Lower Elementary–Intermediate

I	Intermediate
I-UE	Intermediate–Upper Elementary
UE	Upper Elementary

SECONDARY DIVISION
(Books for Young Adults)

Coding

JH	Junior High
JH-SH	Junior High–Senior High
SH	Senior High

Within each of the stated Divisions, the compilers have grouped the entries into categories based upon broad *subject* or *interest* areas. It is possible for a title to be appropriate for one or more categories. When this is indicated, a cross-reference is made. Alphabetical arrangement by author is made for the selections. Complete author, title, and subject indexes give the immediate location of each entry by page number.

Librarians will find particularly helpful the citation of the professional source in which a book is reviewed or listed. These sources and their abbreviations are as follows:

B	*ALA Booklist*
BC	*Books for Children*
C	*Children's Catalog*
CCB	*Bulletin of the Center of Children's Books*
EE	*Elementary English*
ES	*Elementary School Library Collection*
HB	*Horn Book*
JH	*Junior High School Library Catalog*
LJ	*Library Journal*
SH	*Standard Catalog for High School Libraries*
NYT	*New York Times Book Review*

BIBLIOGRAPHY

PICTURE BOOKS

BEIM, LORRAINE. Two Is A Team. Harcourt, Brace & World, 1945. $2.75 (C)

Considered almost a "standard" in intergroup relations, this is a picture story of two small boys, Negro and white, who find it fun to work and play together. Easy vocabulary for primary grades.

LE

ETS, MARIE HALL. See Tarry, Ellen, page 6.

GRIFALCONI, ANN. City Rhythms. Bobbs-Merrill, 1965. $4.95 (ES)

Both the text and the illustrations convey the vitality, movement, and exuberance of city life. Excellent material for the language arts program.

LE

HAWKINSON, JOHN, and HAWKINSON, LUCY. Little Boy Who Lives Up High. Albert Whitman, 1967. $2.95 (B)

A slight but engaging first-person picture book story in which a small Negro boy describes his view of the world from the window of his high-rise apartment.

LE

HORVATH, BETTY. Hooray for Jasper. Franklin Watts, 1966.
$2.95 (CCB)
> An easy reader, whose hero is a small middle-class Negro boy
> who lives in an admirably integrated community.
> **LE**

KEATS, EZRA J. The Snowy Day. Viking Press, 1962. $3.00
(C)
> A little boy responds to the beauty of snow. The illustrations
> of Negro characters won the 1963 Caldecott Medal.
> **LE**

————. **Whistle for Willie.** Viking Press, 1964. $3.50 (C)
> The engaging little boy of **The Snowy Day** appears again in
> a new and equally satisfying picture story.
> **LE**

KESSLER, LEONARD. Here Comes the Strikeout. Harper &
Row, 1965. $1.95 (ES)
> This simple book for beginning readers combines a good
> baseball story with descriptions of fine interracial relation-
> ships.
> **LE**

LANSDOWN, BRENDA. Galumph. Houghton Mifflin, 1966.
$3.50 (HB)
> An easy reading story about a neighborhood cat who is
> known by different names to four different individuals who
> live in the neighborhood. A tragic event that occurs one
> summer day brings them all together. Text is accompanied
> by illustrations.
> **LE**

MARTIN, PATRICIA M. Little Brown Hen. Thomas Y.
Crowell, 1960. $2.95 (LJ)
> Willie's pet hen has disappeared. To add to the boy's wor-
> ries, he cannot find the ducks he needs for his mother's
> birthday present. When the pet hen is found, she is proudly

clucking over a nest of four ducklings, thus solving all Willie's problems. Illustrations show that the characters are Negroes.
LE

ROCKWELL, ANNE. **Gypsy Girl's Best Shoes.** Parents' Magazine, 1966. $3.50 (CCB)
A read-aloud book with illustrations in small, bright detail of vivid scenes of New York City and of the colorful racial and ethnic hodge-podge of some neighborhoods.
LE

SCOTT, ANN HERBERT. **Big Cowboy Western.** Lothrop, Lee & Shepard, 1965. Illustrated by Richard Lewis. $2.95 (ES)
A small Negro boy gets a cowboy suit for his birthday and becomes the biggest cowboy in town.
LE
————. **Sam.** McGraw-Hill, 1967. $3.95 (LJ)
The illustrations poignantly reflect Sam's disappointment at the rebuffs of his family and portray the varying moods of the Negro characters.
LE

SHACKELFORD, JANE D. **My Happy Days.** Associated Publishers, 1944. $2.65
In photographs and simple text, the book describes the daily experiences of a little Negro boy.
LE

SHARPE, STELLA GENTRY. **Tobe.** University of North Carolina Press, 1939. $3.00 (B)
The illustrations and text of this book describe the daily routine of a rural Negro family and of a little boy named Tobe.
LE

STANLEY, JOHN. It's Nice to Be Little. Rand McNally, 1965. $2.75 (LJ)

The story of four children, one of whom is a Negro, and their experiences of growing and wishing to be bigger.
LE

TARRY, ELLEN, and ETS, MARIE HALL. My Dog Rinty. Viking Press, 1946. Photographs by Alexander and Alexandra Alland. $3.00 (C)

A boy and his dog explore their Harlem neighborhood, sometimes creating havoc, but most times just having fun.
LE

UDRY, JANICE. What Mary Jo Shared. Albert Whitman, 1966. $2.95 (B)

A shy little Negro girl thinks her father, a high school teacher, is just right for sharing during show-and-tell time.
LE

FICTION

Elementary

BAKER, BETTY. Walk The World's Rim. Harper & Row, 1965. $3.95 (NYT)
>The central character in this distinguished piece of historical fiction is the Negro slave, Esteban, who was one of the four survivors of the disastrous Narvaez Expedition to Florida in 1527.
>**I-UE**

BAUM, BETTY. Patricia Crosses Town. Alfred A. Knopf, 1965. $3.50 (CCB)
>Pat, twelve, doesn't want to be one of the small group of Negro children who are going to be enrolled in a school across town in an all-white neighborhood, but her parents insist. The book has a worthy aim and a candid approach to the Negro child's view of the stresses of integration.
>**I-UE**

BONHAM, FRANK. Mystery of the Fat Cat. E. P. Dutton, 1968. $3.95 (LJ)
>A very funny mystery story of Buddy Williams, his friends, and their Boys Club located in Dogtown.
>**UE**

————. **The Nitty Gritty.** E. P. Dutton, 1968. $3.95

The story of Charlie Matthews, who lives in Dogtown, a ghetto in a large city. Charlie gains new insights when he runs away from home with his Uncle Baron.

UE

BONTEMPS, ARNA. Lonesome Boy. Houghton Mifflin, 1967. $3.25 (NYT)

Autobiographical illustrations of the lonesome boy theme. Highly realistic story.

LE-I

BRODSKY, MIMI. The House at 12 Rose Street. Abelard-Schuman, 1966. $3.50 (NYT)

The action centers around a Boy Scout Troop torn between following the leadership of Stretch, a boy with violent racial prejudice, or his best friend, Bobby, who doesn't understand why the color of a person's skin matters.

UE

CARLSON, NATALIE S. Ann Aurelia and Dorothy. Harper & Row, 1968. $3.95 (NYT)

Ann Aurelia is a boyish-looking waif who has lived in a succession of foster homes. Her best friend is a cheerful Negro girl, Dorothy Grant. They have a series of predictable adventures, trick-or-treating on Halloween and experimenting with weird concoctions in Dorothy's mother's kitchen.

UE

————. **The Empty Schoolhouse.** Harper & Row, 1965. $3.95 (ES)

Winner of the 1965 Children's Book Award of the Child Study Association of America, this is the story of a young girl who faces the uncertainties of integrating a formerly all-white school. Effective handling of a difficult theme, which thoughtful elementary pupils should find interesting. Illustrations are good and add to the impact of the story.

LE-I

CHANDLER, RUTH F. Ladder to the Sky. Abelard-Schuman, 1965. $3.50 (HB)

> The problems of a Negro family living in a predominantly white Northern community are told simply and directly. The hero of the story is thirteen-year-old Chip who is not academically successful as a seventh-grader.
> **UE**

CONE, MOLLY. The Other Side of the Fence. Houghton Mifflin, 1967. $3.25 (CCB)

> The story of Joey's attempts to welcome the new neighbors who happen to be Negro.
> **LE-I**

DE ANGELI, MARGUERITE. Bright April. Doubleday, 1964. $3.50 (HB)

> Living in a community where she has always been accepted without question, April begins to experience the hurt that can be caused by prejudice. But a wise family, an understanding scout leader, and happy school experiences make it possible for April to find happiness.
> **I-UE**

DESBARATS, PETER. Gabrielle and Selena. Harcourt, Brace & World, 1968. $2.95. (LJ)

> An interesting story depicting family life of two eight-year-old girls; one is white and the other is Negro.
> **LE-I**

DOUGLAS, MARJORY S. Freedom River. Charles Scribner's Sons, 1953. $3.95 (B)

> A Negro slave, a Seminole Indian, and a white Quaker boy solve their problems together against the background of the slave-state question in Florida.
> **UE**

FAULKNER, GEORGENE. Melindy's Medal. Julian Messner, 1945. $3.50; paper $.50 (ES)

A different pattern of family life is portrayed in this interesting story about an eight-year-old Negro girl. She won her medal for "just pure bravery."

I

————. **Melindy's Happy Summer.** Julian Messner, 1947. $3.50 (ES)

In this sequel to **Melindy's Medal,** Melindy visits Maine, where she enjoys life on a big farm. A good portrayal of family life.

I

FIFE, DALE. Who's in Charge of Lincoln? Coward-McCann, 1965. Illustrated by Paul Galdone. $2.86 (ES)

The writing style is easy although the plot is a little far-fetched. Will be enjoyed by Negro children, who are seldom heroes in the books they read.

I

GRAHAM, LORENZ. South Town. Follett, 1960. $3.95 (ES)

Deals with the struggle of a poor Negro family to improve its way of life. The book interprets effectively the relationships between Negroes and whites. The sequel, **North Town,** deals with the fortunes of the same family after moving North.

I-UE

HAMILTON, VIRGINIA. Zeely. Macmillan, 1967. $3.95 (LJ)

A beautiful story of the relationship between Zeely, who resembles a Watusi princess, and Geeder, who is visiting her uncle's farm. Will appeal especially to girls feeling growing pains.

I-UE

HENTOFF, NAT. Jazz Country. Harper & Row, 1965. $3.50;
Dell paper $.50
> Realistic portrayal of the Negro world of jazz as experienced
> by a teenage white boy who wishes to become a trumpet
> player.
> **UE**

HILBERT, PETER PAUL. Zoo on the First Floor. Coward-
McCann, 1967. $3.50 (LJ)
> Written in the first person, this is the story of one summer's
> activities of a boy, his mother, sister, and Napoleon, a
> Negro friend.
> **I-UE**

HILL, ELIZABETH. Evan's Corner. Holt, Rinehart & Winston, 1966. $3.95 (HB)
> A young boy finally gets a place of his own in a two-room
> flat where he lives with his parents, three sisters and two
> brothers, only to find that something is still missing.
> **LE-I**

HORVATH, BETTY. Hooray for Jasper.
> See page 4.

HUNT, MABEL LEIGH. Ladycake Farm. J. B. Lippincott,
1952. $3.25 (C)
> A story of a Negro family who move to a farm in a previ-
> ously all-white neighborhood. The family experiences sev-
> eral difficulties before they are accepted.
> **I-UE**

JACKSON, JESSE. Call Me Charley. Harper & Row, 1945. $2.95;
Dell paper $.65 (ES, C)
> This title has long been a favorite on intercultural book lists.
> It is the story of the first Negro boy in the local school and
> how his athletic prowess wins him a place of leadership and
> respect.
> **UE**

JUSTUS, MAY. New Home for Billy. Hastings House, 1966. $3.25 (ES)

> A simple story of a Negro family who leave their tenement dwelling in a ghetto to settle in a run-down house in the country.
> **LE-I**

KEATS, EZRA J. Peter's Chair. Harper & Row, 1967. $3.95 (LJ)

> The story of Peter's rebellion when he feels that his place in the family has been usurped by the new baby. An excellent study of sibling rivalry.
> **LE-I**

KONIGSBURG, E. L. Jennifer, Hecate, Macbeth, William McKinley and Me Elizabeth. Atheneum, 1967. $3.50 (LJ)

> Two lonely girls—one a witch, the other her apprentice—are drawn together in an interracial friendship.
> **I-UE**

LEVY, MIMI C. Corrie and the Yankee. Viking Press, 1959. $3.00 (ES)

> Corrie, a slave, helps an escaped and wounded white soldier to safety through the Underground Railroad. This is a good recreational book for elementary and junior high grades and may serve as an introduction to the study of Negroes and slavery in America.
> **UE**

LEWIS, RICHARD W. A Summer Adventure. Harper & Row, 1962. $2.95

> There is nothing in the story nor in the speech of the characters to indicate that this is a Negro family. Only the attractive illustrations portray this fact.
> **I-UE**

LEXAU, JOAN M. Benjie. Dial Press, 1964. $3.00 (LJ)
Benjie is a shy Negro youngster who overcomes his problem when he finds his grandmother's earring.
LE-I

———. **Striped Ice Cream.** J. B. Lippincott, 1968. $3.25 (LJ)
A story about a real family—the ups and downs, the quarrels and making-ups. Best of all, it is the story of Becky's birthday and a happy surprise.
LE-I

LIPKIND, WILLIAM, and MORDVINOFF, NICOLAS. Four-Leaf Clover. Harcourt, Brace & World, 1959. $3.50 (LJ)
Two boys, one white and one Negro, search for a four-leaf clover because they can use a little luck. Their search is successful, funny, and breathlessly exciting, but their greatest luck is that they are friends.
I-UE

LIPSYTE, ROBERT. The Contender. Harper & Row, 1967. $3.50
After dropping out of school, Alfred decides the only way to make it out of Harlem is to work at being a great fighter.
UE

MILES, MISKA. Mississippi Possum. Little, Brown, 1965. $3.00 (HB)
Life on the lower Mississippi sometimes involves being flooded out of one's home. When this happens to the Jackson family, they take refuge at the top of the hill. Among the evacuees is a shy, frightened possum, who is befriended by Rose Mary and Jefferson Jackson. The attractive illustrations, showing that the Jacksons are Negroes, are by John Schoenheer.
I

MILLENDER, DHARATHULA. Crispus Attucks: Boy of Valor. Bobbs-Merrill, 1965. $2.50 (CCB)

A fictionalized biography of the Negro hero of the Revolutionary War. Most of the book is concerned with Attucks' childhood, but traces his adult years briefly.

I

MORDVINOFF, NICOLAS. See Lipkind, William, page 13.

MORSE, EVANGELINE. Brown Rabbit: Her Story. Follett, 1967. $3.50 (NYT)

A Negro family's experiences in leaving a pleasant but hopelessly second-class life in a Southern college town and moving to the ugly, congested, but potentially better world of a Northern city.

LE-I

PALMER, CANDIDA. Snow Storm Before Christmas. J. B. Lippincott, 1965. $2.75

The story of two Negro boys and the experiences they share while shopping for Christmas gifts for their mother and sister.

LE-I

————. **A Ride on High.** J. B. Lippincott, 1966. $2.95

The story of two Negro boys and their exciting ride on the elevated train.

LE-I

PETERSON, JOHN. Enemies of the Secret Hide-out. Four Winds Press, 1966. $2.50 (LJ)

Using a very simple plot and vocabulary, Mr. Peterson has managed to create a realistic adventure story for young boys.

LE-I

RAFTERY, GERALD. Twenty-Dollar Horse. Julian Messner, 1955. $2.64

> Two young boys, one white and one Negro, share a horse. The adventure, as well as the racial prejudice they encounter, helps to strengthen their community.
>
> **UE**

SHOTWELL, LOUISA. Roosevelt Grady. World, 1963. $2.95; Grosset paper $.50 (ES)

> The author describes with sympathy and understanding the problems of a Negro family who could well be members of any other ethnic group. The illustrations by Peter Burchard are very attractive.
>
> **I**

———. **Adam Bookout,** Viking Press, 1967. $3.95 (LJ)

> Eleven-year-old Adam runs away from home in Oklahoma to Brooklyn after the death of his parents. In Brooklyn he comes to understand that running away does not solve problems.
>
> **I-UE**

STOLZ, MARY. Noon Day Friends. Harper & Row, 1965. $3.95; Grosset paper $.50 (HB)

> This story is told with the candor and forthrightness of eleven-year-olds, and with insights into the warmth and humor of some families under the most deplorable conditions.
>
> **I-UE**

———. **A Wonderful, Terrible Time.** Harper & Row, 1967 $3.79 (HB)

> A story of two Negro girls, Sue Ellen and Mady, and their experiences of growing up in the city.
>
> **I-UE**

Secondary

BALDWIN, JAMES. Go Tell It On The Mountain. Dial Press, 1963. $4.50; Dell paper $.60 (SH)

> A novel about growing up in Harlem before World War II.
>
> **SH**

BARRETT, WILLIAM E. Lilies of the Field. Doubleday, 1962. $2.95 (B)

A pleasant novel of a young Negro recently discharged from the Army. He finds himself building a chapel for a small group of German nuns.
JH-SH

BAUM, BETTY. Patricia Crosses Town.
See page 7.

BENNETT, HAL. Black Wine. Doubleday, 1968. $4.95; Pyramid paper $.75 (LJ)

The story of David Hunter's boyhood presents an informative reflection of the matriarchal society of modern Negro culture.
SH

BLANTON, CATHERINE. Hold Fast to Your Dreams. Julian Messner, 1955. $3.50; paper $.50 (JH)

Because of her dark skin, a talented young dancer faces prejudice and discrimination in her struggle to achieve. Useful for "courage" unit.
JH-SH

BONTEMPS, ARNA. Chariot in the Sky: A Story of the Jubilee Singers. Holt, Rinehart & Winston, 1951. $3.27 (SH)

This historical novel has special meaning because it deals with the important discovery of the beauty and richness of the Negro spirituals.
JH-SH

BRADBURY, BIANCA. Lots of Love. Ives Washburn, 1966. $3.50 (LJ)

Lucinda, a Negro Alabaman, spends her junior year with the Lee family in their very prim and proper white Connecticut community.
JH-SH

————. **The Undergrounders.** Ives Washburn, 1966. $2.95 (ES)
The story has overtones of today's social problems as it
touches on the pros and cons of church involvement and
on the relevance of law (in this case the Fugitive Slave Law)
to a teaching that one considers unjust.
JH-SH

BRODSKY, MIMI. The House at 12 Rose Street.
See page 8.

BROWIN, FRANCES. Looking for Orlando. Criterion Books,
1961. $3.50 (HB)
Good characterization, moral values, exciting action, and
pleasant romance combine to form an adventure story about
the Underground Railroad.
JH

CARLSON, NATALIE S. Ann Aurelia and Dorothy.
See page 8.

CAVANNA, BETTY. A Time for Tenderness. William Morrow,
1962. $3.50; Berkley Publishing paper $.50
A white girl from North Carolina goes to Brazil for one year
and falls in love. She and her brother find interracial relationships in that country different from those in the United
States.
JH

CHANDLER, RUTH F. Ladder to the Sky.
See page 9.

CLARKE, JOHN HENRIK (editor). **American Negro Short
Stories.** Hill and Wang, 1966. $5.95; paper $1.95 (LJ)
Thirty-one stories culled from different periodicals and
books represent a cross section of the life of Negroes in the
United States. Contributors range from Paul Laurence Dun-

bar and Charles W. Chestnut to Lerone Bennett, Jr., and James Baldwin. Section of "Biographical Notes" on all authors.
JH-SH

COLMAN, HILA. Classmates by Request. William Morrow, 1964. $3.50 (JH)
The development of friendships across racial lines is one of the positive accomplishments of pupils' efforts at brotherhood. Good for discussion groups in junior high school.
JH

DE LEEUW, ADELE. The Barred Road. Macmillan, 1954. $3.74 (B)
Sue Trowbridge tries to do something about the social problems she meets when she sees how her Negro classmates are treated by some of the teachers and students in her school.
JH-SH

DOUGLAS, MARJORY S. Freedom River.
See page 9.

ELLISON, RALPH. The Invisible Man. Random House, 1952. $5.95; New American Library paper $.95 (SH)
A distinguished adult novel in which the author points up the fact that in order to identify themselves, Negroes must contend with members of their own race as well as with whites. National Book Award winner.
SH

FAIR, RONALD L. Hog Butcher. Harcourt, Brace & World, 1966. $4.50 (SH)
After seeing his teenage athlete hero shot down by policemen in a Chicago ghetto, ten-year-old Wilford must decide whether to tell the truth or yield to adult pressure to remain silent.
SH

FAST, HOWARD. Freedom Road. Crown, 1944. $1.45 (HB)
  Historical novel based on the Reconstruction period in the South following the Civil War, when for a few years Negroes and whites worked together in harmony.
  SH

FORD, JESSE HILL. The Liberation of Lord Byron Jones.
Little, Brown, 1965. $5.95; New American Library paper $.95 (SH)
  A brutally realistic novel of the contemporary racial issues in a small Southern town. Recommended for advanced high school students.
  SH

GAULT, WILLIAM CAMPBELL. Backfield Challenge. E. P. Dutton, 1967. $3.50 (CCB)
  Link, who is Negro, expects trouble when he transfers to a middle-class school in which the star of the football team is prejudiced.
  JH-SH

GRAHAM, LORENZ. North Town. Thomas Y. Crowell, 1965. $3.95
  David Williams' story is typical of the Negro teenager today. David, along with his family, experiences the effects of bigotry and many other problems when they leave South Town.
  JH-SH
——. **South Town.**
  See page 10.

GRAHAM, SHIRLEY. There Was Once a Slave. Julian Messner, 1947. $3.95 (B)
  This is the heroic story of Frederick Douglass, a slave who escaped from bondage, educated himself and became one of the leaders of the abolition movement.
  JH-SH

HAAS, BEN. Look Away, Look Away. Simon & Schuster, 1964.
$5.95; Pocket Books $.75 (JH)

> As youngsters, Carey Bradham, white, and Houston Whit-
> ley, Negro, had been deeply attached, but when they return
> from World War II, Carey becomes dedicated to the preser-
> vation of the way of life that will assure him a career in poli-
> tics. While Houston takes the first steps that will make him a
> leader in the civil rights movement, Carey moves toward the
> governorship and becomes involved with segregationists.
> **SH**

————. **The Troubled Summer.** Bobbs-Merrill, 1966. $4.00
(NYT)

> Clay Williams is a Negro high school student who resents the
> binds of segregation. When he is beaten by two Klansmen,
> his resentment becomes a violent but contained hatred.
> **JH-SH**

**HENNESSY, MAURICE, and SAUTER, EDWIN, JR. A Crown
for Thomas Peters.** Ives Washburn, 1964. $3.25

> Captured by the British in the eighteenth century, Thomas
> Peters is sold into slavery in Charleston, South Carolina.
> From that time on he tries to free himself and as many of his
> people as he can, until he finally achieves his dream of re-
> turning to Sierra Leone and becomes mayor of his home
> town.
> **JH-SH**

HENTOFF, NAT. Jazz Country.

> See page 11.

**HUGHES, LANGSTON. The Best Short Stories by Negro
Writers.** Little, Brown, 1966. $7.95 (LJ)

> Included in the collection are representative stories by Ralph
> Ellison, James Baldwin, Richard Wright, and Langston
> Hughes. A vivid and dramatic social history of the Negro
> American in fiction.
> **SH**

————. **Simple's Uncle Sam.** Hill and Wang, 1965. $3.95; paper $1.50 (SH)

> Forty-six stories about Hughes's famous character, Jesse B. Simple, who discusses current affairs.
> SH

JACKSON, JESSE. Call Me Charley.

> See page 11.

JOHNSON, JAMES WELDON. The Autobiography of an Ex-Coloured Man. Alfred A. Knopf, 1955. $3.95; Hill and Wang $1.95 (B)

> A novel that reads like a composite autobiography of the Negro race in the United States in modern times.
> SH

JONES, LEROI. Black Music. William Morrow, 1967. $5.00 (C)

> A collection of short stories concerning the author, his parents, his college years at Howard University, his writer's romance with words and literature, the growing alienation of his years in the Air Force, and the problem of thinking white and being black.
> SH

KELLEY, WILLIAM M. A Different Drummer. Doubleday, 1962. $3.95 (LJ)

> Tucker Caliham, a Negro in the Deep South, decides to follow the teachings of Thoreau. He refuses to participate in a society of such inequalities as he has experienced. Finally, he moves North to a new life after destroying his farm land and his farm animals. Other Negroes follow. The story tells of the effect on the lives of the whites that are left behind
> SH

KILLENS, JOHN O. And Then We Heard the Thunder. Alfred A. Knopf, 1962. $5.95; Pocket Books paper $.75 (SH)
> How a Negro soldier in World War II becomes progressively involved in the battle for equality.
> **SH**

LEVY, MIMI C. Corrie and the Yankee.
> See page 12.

LIPSYTE, ROBERT T. The Contender.
> See page 13.

MADDUX, RACHEL. Abel's Daughter. Harper & Row, 1960. $3.50 (B)
> During the war Ted and Molly Demerest, a young Army couple, come to know and like Abel Loftis, a Negro grocer, and his daughter, Serena. The story of an interracial friendship in the Deep South.
> **SH**

MANTEL, S. G. Tallmadge's Terry. David McKay, 1965. $3.95
> Fifteen-year-old Terry and his friend, Joshua London, a runaway slave, enlist in Lieutenant Tallmadge's regiment to spy on the British for George Washington and fight in the battle of Long Island.
> **JH-SH**

MARSHALL, CATHERINE. Julie's Heritage. David McKay, 1957. $4.50 (B)
> The influence of prejudice and discrimination upon two young Negro pupils is the theme of this junior high novel set in a Northern city. The differences in each pupil's reactions will cause young readers to pause and reflect.
> **JH**

MATHER, MELISSA. One Summer In Between. Harper & Row, 1967. $4.95

As part of her college sociology course, Harriet comes North for the summer to be a mother's helper in a large white family. She gradually learns that real human beings live behind the white faces.

JH-SH

MILLER, WARREN. Cool World. Little, Brown, 1959. $4.75; Fawcett paper $.60 (SH, B)

New York's Harlem, with its dope addicts, delinquents, and gang warfare, is the setting for this powerful novel about fourteen-year-old Duke Curtis, leader of the Royal Crocodiles, who seeks to find money to buy a .45.

SH

NEWELL, HOPE. A Cap for Mary Ellis. Harper & Row, 1953. $3.50 (LJ)

The story of two young girls, enrolled in an all-Negro school of nursing, who are chosen to represent their race in a private school experimenting with interracial classes.

JH-SH

————. **Mary Ellis, Student Nurse.** Harper & Row, 1958. $3.50; Berkley paper $.50 (HB)

Two Negro girls are the first members of their race to integrate a nursing school. An experience that they fear turns out to be a pleasant part of their lives.

JH

PARKS, GORDON. The Learning Tree. Harper & Row, 1963. $4.95 (LJ)

A charming story of a year in the life of a Negro boy growing up in a small Kansas town in the 1920's.

SH

PETRY, ANN. Tituba of Salem Village. Thomas Y. Crowell, 1964. $4.50 (HB)

> Tituba, a Negro slave woman, is one of the first three persons to be condemned in the Salem Witch Trials of 1692. Historical fiction based on reports of testimony from the trials.
> **JH-SH**

RODMAN, BELLA, Lions In The Way. Follett, 1966. $3.95; Avon paper $.60 (LJ)

> "I thought I heard them say/There were lions in the way." These words from a spiritual express the courage of Negro teenagers in desegregating a Tennessee high school.
> **JH-SH**

SANGUINETTI, ELSIE. The New Girl. McGraw-Hill, 1964. $6.50 (LJ)

> A warm, sometimes funny, entertaining story that touches on the changing racial attitudes in the South and covers many events in Felicia's life at school.
> **JH-SH**

SAUTER, EDWIN, JR. See Hennessy, Maurice, page 20.

STERLING, DOROTHY. Mary Jane. Doubleday, 1959. $3.50 (HB)

> A perceptive story of a Negro girl's adjustment at a newly integrated junior high school.
> **JH**

WALKER, MARGARET. Jubilee. Houghton Mifflin. $5.95 (LJ)

> Story of life on a Georgia plantation from the Civil War to the Reconstruction period. A Houghton Mifflin Literary Fellowship Award Novel.
> **SH**

WHEELER, KEITH. Peaceable Lane. Simon & Schuster, 1960. $4.50 (B)

A novel about a Negro's decision to move into an exclusive New York suburb.

SH

NONFICTION

THE ARTS

Elementary

EATON, JEANETTE. Trumpeter's Tale: The Story of Young Louis Armstrong. William Morrow, 1955. $3.95 (B)
> The biography of one of America's famous Negro jazz musicians.
> **I-UE**

HUGHES, LANGSTON. Famous Negro Music Makers. Dodd, Mead, 1955. $3.50
> A collection of brief biographies of sixteen Negro musicians and of The Jubilee Singers.
> **I-UE**

LANDECK, BEATRICE. Echoes of Africa in Folk Songs of the Americas. David McKay, 1961. $5.95 (B)
> A well-known musicologist traces folk music and jazz from Africa to the Americas
> **I-UE**

ROLLINS, CHARLEMAE H. Famous Negro Entertainers. Dodd, Mead, 1967. $3.50 (JH)

> Popular show business personalities, such as Louis Armstrong, Lena Horne, Sidney Poitier, and the late Nat King Cole.
>
> **UE**

Secondary

ANDERSON, MARIAN. My Lord, What a Morning. Viking, 1966. $5.00; Avon paper $.60 (SH)

> The autobiography of the famous American singer describes her Philadelphia childhood and her successes at home and abroad.
>
> **JH-SH**

CHARTERS, SAMUEL BARCLAY. The Bluesmen: The Story and the Music of the Men Who Made the Blues. Oak Publications, 1967. $6.95; paper $3.95 (LJ)

> The primary emphasis in this book is on the personalities and styles of the Mississippi region—the most important geographical area in the development of the blues. The history of important bluesmen is given, along with a description of their playing and singing styles.
>
> **SH**

COURLANDER, HAROLD. Negro Folk Music, U.S.A. Columbia University Press, 1963. $10.00 (LJ)

> A discussion of the development of Negro folk music—vocal and instrumental—in general non-technical terms.
>
> **JH-SH**

CUNEY-HARE, MAUD. Negro Musicians and Their Music. Associated Publishers, 1936. $4.00 (B)

> Negro contributions to music, from the African origins to the present-day Negro American songs. An appendix gives historical information on African musical instruments.
>
> **JH-SH**

DAVIS, SAMMY, JR. Yes, I Can. Farrar, Straus, 1965. $6.95 (B)

> The autobiography of a versatile entertainer of movies, TV, and stage.
> **SH**

DE TREVINO, ELIZABETH. I, Juan de Pareja. Farrar, Straus, 1965. $3.25 (LJ)

> An absorbing biographical novel based on the life of Juan de Pareja, the Negro slave of Velasquez, the famous Spanish artist. Stimulating material for art history and for intercultural relations, also for world history classes. Winner of the Newbery Medal for 1966.
> **JH-SH**

DOVER, CEDRIC. American Negro Art. 3rd ed. New York Graphic Society, 1965. $12.00 (JH)

> A richly stimulating introduction to the work of major Negro American artists up to the present. The book covers all types of art: painting, sculpture, crafts, ceramics, etc.
> **JH-SH**

EATON, JEANETTE. Trumpeter's Tale: The Story of Young Louis Armstrong.

> See page 26.

HOYT, EDWIN PALMER. Paul Robeson: The American Othello. World, 1967. $5.95 (LJ)

> This is a sensitive biography concentrating on the political development of Paul Robeson, the great American Negro actor-singer who climbed the heights of his profession.
> **SH**

HUGHES, LANGSTON. Famous Negro Music Makers. Dodd, Mead, 1955. $3.50

> See page 26.

———. **First Book of Jazz.** Franklin Watts, 1954. $2.65 (HB)

> A simple explanation of the evolution of jazz, plus a brief

description of famous jazz musicians. There is also a list of suggested recordings.
JH

HUGHES, LANGSTON, and MELTZER, MILTON. Black Magic: A Pictorial History of the Negro in American Entertainment. Prentice-Hall, 1968. $10.00 (LJ)
The late poet laureate of the Negro people here combines his talents with an expert in graphic history and biography to create a panorama of history—tracing the development of the Negro contribution to American entertainment.
SH

JACKSON, MAHALIA, and WYLIE, E. M. Movin' On Up: The Mahalia Jackson Story. Hawthorn Books, 1966. $5.95 (SH)
A famous gospel singer tells of her hardships and successes and of the simple faith that has kept her "movin' on up."
JH-SH

JOHNSON, JAMES WELDON, and J. ROSAMOND. The Book of American Negro Spirituals. Viking Press, 1940. $6.95 (SH)
The first and second volumes of American Negro Spirituals have been combined in this one volume. Many of the songs are difficult but the arrangements by J. Rosamond Johnson have made them favorites for years.
SH

JONES, LEROI. Blues People: Negro Music In White America. William Morrow, 1963. $5.00; Apollo paper $1.65 (LJ)
An exploration of the Negro American's music, from the slave songs to "cool" jazz, shows how its continuum coincides with his cultural history as an American.
SH

KIRKEBY, EDWARD. Ain't Misbehavin': The Story of Fats Waller. Dodd, Mead, 1966. $5.00 (LJ)

An appreciative and critical biography of the famous pianist, singer, and composer of the Thirties.
SH

LANDECK, BEATRICE. Echoes of Africa in Folk Songs of the Americas.
See page 26.

MELTZER, MILTON. See Hughes, Langston, page 29.

NATHAN, HANS. Dan Emmett and the Rise of Early Minstrelsy. University of Oklahoma Press, 1962. $10.00 (SH)
A basic work on the influence Negroes have had on American music.
SH

NEWMAN, SHIRLEE. Marian Anderson: Lady from Philadelphia. Westminster Press, 1966. $3.75 (ES)
Deep faith, perseverance, devotion to family and music, dignity in the face of insult and discrimination are portrayed in this uplifting biography.
JH-SH

ROBESON, ESLANDA G. Paul Robeson, Negro. Harper & Row, 1930. $2.50 (B)
Story of the early life and career of the Negro actor and singer, as told by his wife.
SH

ROLLINS, CHARLEMAE. Famous Negro Entertainers.
See page 27.

SHAW, ARNOLD. Belafonte. Chilton Books, 1960. $3.50 (B)
The biography of one of America's most famous folk singers.
SH

TERKEL, STUDS. Giants of Jazz. Thomas Y. Crowell, 1957. $3.50 (B)
Informative and entertaining sketches of several Negro jazz musicians.
JH-SH

WYLIE, E. M. See Jackson, Mahalia, page 29.

LITERATURE

AUTHORS

Elementary

GOULD, JEAN. That Dunbar Boy. Dodd, Mead, 1958. $3.25 (HB)
The author does not attempt an evaluation of Paul Laurence Dunbar's work, but rather presents an interesting account of a Negro poet who made a unique contribution to American literature.
I-UE

GRAHAM, SHIRLEY. The Story of Phillis Wheatley. Julian Messner, 1949. $3.50 (ES)
The fascinating story of the Negro poetess "from the day she was rescued from the Boston slave market by the kindly Mrs. Wheatley until her death in 1784."
I-UE

Secondary

FERGUSON, BLANCH E. Countee Cullen and the Negro Renaissance. Dodd, Mead, 1966. $5.00 (LJ)
> This biography sheds much light on the well-known poet who portrayed the Harlem of the Twenties.
> **JH-SH**

GOULD, JEAN. That Dunbar Boy.
> See page 31.

GRAHAM, SHIRLEY. The Story of Phillis Wheatley.
> See page 31.

HUGHES, LANGSTON. The Big Sea. Hill and Wang, 1963. $4.50; paper $1.95 (SH)
> The autobiography of Langston Hughes.
> **SH**
————. **I Wonder as I Wander.** Hill and Wang, 1964. $4.95; paper $2.65 (SH)
> A sequel to Hughes's **The Big Sea.**
> **SH**

JOHNSON, JAMES WELDON. Along This Way. Viking Press, 1933. $7.50 (SH)
> The classic autobiography of a distinguished Negro; sensitively written, witty, philosophical, and humorous.
> **SH**

ROLLINS, CHARLEMAE H. Famous American Negro Poets. Dodd, Mead, 1965. $3.50 (CCB)
> Anecdotal biography of twelve American Negro poets, from Jupiter Hammon and Phillis Wheatley to Langston Hughes and Gwendolyn Brooks, with samples of their poetry.
> **JH-SH**

•

BIBLIOGRAPHY

•

TARRY, ELLEN. Young Jim: The Early Years of James Weldon Johnson. Dodd, Mead, 1967. $3.75

A well-written presentation of how Johnson became the outstanding figure he is in almost every aspect of American cultural and social history.

JH-SH

WEBB, CONSTANCE. Biography of Richard Wright. G. P. Putnam's Sons, 1968. $8.95 (LJ)

A book about Wright that is a combination of personal reminiscences, scholarship, and literary appraisal.

SH

WRIGHT, RICHARD. Black Boy. Harper & Row, 1945. Paper $.75 (B)

The author, one of the important writers of the Thirties, tells of his rugged boyhood in Chicago.

JH-SH

CRITICISM

Secondary

BALDWIN, JAMES. Notes of a Native Son. Beacon Press, 1957. $1.45; Dial, 1963. $4.50 (SH)

Essays that relate the author's boyhood and growing-up in Harlem and his feelings on being a Negro in a large American city. Also included, and perhaps most significant, are his commentaries on literature and the performing arts.

SH

ELLISON, RALPH. Shadow and Act. Random House, 1964. $5.59; New American Library paper $.95 (LJ)

A collection of essays concerned with American literature, folklore, and musical expression.

SH

EMANUEL, JAMES A. Langston Hughes. Twayne, 1967. $3.95

A much-needed appraisal of Langston Hughes's literary work.

SH

GLOSTER, HUGH M. Negro Voices in American Fiction. Russell & Russell, 1965. $7.50 (SH)

Glimpses into the social history of Negro Americans through a treatment of Negro fiction from World War I up to the Thirties. A revision of a book first published in 1948.

SH

GROSS, SEYMOUR L., and HARDY, J. E. (editors). Images of the Negro in American Literature. University of Chicago Press, 1966. $6.50; paper $2.95 (SH)

Critical essays that present the changing image of Negroes in American fiction from colonial America to the present time.

SH

HARDY, J. E. See Gross, Seymour L., page 34.

HILL, HERBERT (editor). Anger, and Beyond. Harper & Row, 1966. $5.95 (SH)

A collection of critical essays on the writing of Negro Americans.

SH

WILLIAMS, JOHN A. (compiler). Beyond the Angry Black. Cooper Square, 1968. $5.50

Nineteen contributors discuss the Negro in this country through poems, essays, fiction, and drama.

SH

DRAMA

BALDWIN, JAMES. Blues for Mr. Charlie. Dial Press, 1964. $3.95; Dell paper $.60 (LJ)
> A young Negro who has lived in the North and has become a drug addict returns home and is killed by a white Southerner. The play looks at the ways in which both whites and Negroes contributed to his death.
> **SH**

DUBERMAN, MARTIN B. In White America: A Documentary Play. Houghton Mifflin, 1964. $3.95; paper $1.75; New American Library paper $.60 (SH)
> A social problem presented in dramatic form, which seeks to show that Negroes have become militant through deprivation, and that solutions of the social ills are long overdue. Lengthy notes and episodic form make it more suitable for reading than acting.
> **SH**

HANSBERRY, LORRAINE. A Raisin in the Sun. Random House, 1959. $4.50 (SH)
> A heartwarming drama of what happens when a Negro tenement family in Chicago receives the legacy of an insurance policy.
> **JH-SH**

HUGHES, LANGSTON. Five Plays. Edited by Webster Smalley. Indiana University Press, 1963. $5.95 (SH)
> Selections are "Mulatto," "Souls Gone Home," "Little Ham," "Simply Heavenly," and "Tambourines to Glory."
> **SH**

MITCHELL, LOFTEN. Black Drama: The Story of the American Negro in the Theatre. Hawthorn Books, 1968. $5.95 (LJ)
> The author presents a much-needed history of the Negro's role in the American theatre.
> **SH**

POETRY

Elementary

BONTEMPS, ARNA. Golden Slippers: An Anthology of Negro Poetry. Harper & Row, 1941. $3.95 (SH)
> A young people's collection of poetry by Negroes, with brief biographical sketches of the poets.
> **I-UE**

HUGHES, LANGSTON. The Dream Keeper and Other Poems. Alfred A. Knopf, 1932. $2.79 (C)
> A collection of poetry selected expressly for young people. The poetic concepts and reading level will make this reference appealing to the mature elementary reader.
> **I-UE**

JOHNSON, JAMES WELDON. God's Trombones. Viking Press, 1927. $3.75
> Eloquent and dramatic sermons in poetry. Included is the well-known "Creation."
> **UE**

SWIFT, HILDEGARDE H. North Star Shining. William Morrow, 1947. $3.95 (ES)
> A brief history of Negro Americans written in free verse and movingly illustrated with lithographs by Lynd Ward. Crispus Attucks, Harriet Tubman, Frederick Douglass, Joe Louis, and soldiers of World War II are included. An older title that is too good to miss. Excellent read-aloud material as well as independent reading.
> **I-UE**

Secondary

ADOFF, ARNOLD. I Am the Darker Brother: An Anthology of Modern Poems by Negro Americans. Macmillan, 1968. $4.95 (LJ)
> Sixty-four selections by twenty-eight American Negro poets

who reflect on the past, on the current social scene, and on the hope for the future. Helpful biographical sketches and notes on poems of particular interest are included.
JH-SH

BONTEMPS, ARNA. See Hughes, Langston, page 38.
————. **Golden Slippers.**
See page 36.
———— (editor). **American Negro Poetry.** Hill and Wang, 1963. $4.95; paper $1.45 (SH)
An anthology that includes the works of fifty-six poets during the last seventy years.
JH-SH

BROOKS, GWENDOLYN. Selected Poems. Harper & Row, 1963. $3.95; paper $1.65 (LJ)
Selections from her earlier poems in addition to some new ones—mostly about Negro life.
JH-SH

CULLEN, COUNTEE. On These I Stand: An Anthology of the Best Poems. Harper & Row, 1947. $4.95 (SH)
These poems, mostly unfamiliar to students of American literature and almost totally excluded from school anthologies, will be a revelation of the beauty and literary accomplishment frequently found in the work of Negro poets.
SH

DUNBAR, PAUL L. Complete Poems. Apollo paper $1.95 (JH)
The works of one of the earliest Negro poets to achieve wide recognition. Many poems are written in dialect.
JH-SH

HAYDEN, ROBERT (editor). **Kaleidoscope.** Harcourt, Brace & World, 1967. $3.95 (NYT)
A rich anthology of the best American Negro poetry emphasizing literary value rather than social significance.
JH-SH

HUGHES, LANGSTON. The Dream Keeper and Other Poems.
See page 36.
————. **Selected Poems.** Alfred A. Knopf, 1959. $5.00 (SH)
A representative sampling of Hughes's poems.
JH-SH
———— (editor). **New Negro Poets, USA.** Indiana University
Press, 1964. $4.95 (HB, SH)
A collection of poetry by thirty-seven Negro poets—poems
of protest, love, death, humor, description, and prejudice.
JH-SH

HUGHES, LANGSTON, and BONTEMPS, ARNA (editors).
The Poetry of the Negro, 1746–1949. Doubleday, 1951. $6.50 (SH)
While not all of this anthology is the work of Negro American poets, the first section, "Negro Poets of the U. S. A.,"
contains a representative collection of well-known and lesser
known poets of this period.
JH-SH

JOHNSON, JAMES WELDON. God's Trombones.
See page 36.
———— (editor). **American Negro Poetry: An Anthology.** rev. ed.
Harcourt, Brace & World, 1934. $5.50 (SH)
Biographical sketches precede selections of poems by Negro
Americans, from Paul Laurence Dunbar to Langston
Hughes. Works by many lesser known poets are also in-
cluded. The anthology is equally famous for its introductory
essay on "The Creative Genius of the Negro."
JH-SH

TOLSON, MELVIN B. Harlem Gallery. Twayne, 1965. $4.00
(C)
The theme in this long poem is the quandary of Negroes in
American society today. The introduction is by Karl Sha-
piro. An excellent source for readers of experimental verse.
SH

RELIGION

BISHOP, CLAIRE. Martin de Porres, Hero. Houghton Mifflin, 1954. $3.95 (LJ)

    The biography of a seventeenth-century Peruvian Negro who became a saint.

    I-UE-JH

FOLEY, ALBERT, S. God's Men of Color. Farrar, Straus, 1955. $4.50 (LJ)

    A collection of biographies of Negro Roman Catholic priests of the United States from 1854 to 1954.

    JH-SH

FRAZIER, E. FRANKLIN. Negro Church in America. Schocken Books, 1964. $3.50; paper $1.45 (LJ)

    "Published as a tribute to the memory of Professor Frazier, this is an enlargement of a lecture he gave at the University of Liverpool in 1953." Evolution of the Negro church from its beginning to the present. Recommended for the advanced student.

    SH

LINCOLN, C. ERIC. The Black Muslims in America. Beacon Press, 1961. $4.95; paper $1.95 (B)

    After attending meetings and interviewing Muslim leaders, the author gives a sociological analysis of the Nation of Islam movement.

    SH

LOMAX, LOUIS E. When The Word Is Given. New American Library, 1963. Paper $.60 (LJ)

    Popularly written story based on interviews and newspaper articles about the Black Muslims.

    SH

MAYS, BENJAMIN. The Negro's God, As Reflected in His Literature. Chapman and Grimes, 1938. $2.00
> The purpose of the book is to trace historically the development of the idea of God in Negro literature, mass and classical, from 1760 to 1937.
> **SH**

WASHINGTON, JOSEPH R. Black Religion: The Negro and Christianity in the United States. Beacon Press, 1964. $5.00; paper $2.45 (LJ)
> A frank discussion of black and white Christians and their segregated congregations.
> **SH**

YATES, ELIZABETH. Howard Thurman: Portrait of a Practical Dreamer. John Day, 1964. $4.95 (LJ)
> The biography of a leading Negro clergyman who rose from humble beginnings in Florida to become Dean of the Chapel at Boston University.
> **JH-SH**

SCIENCE

Elementary

BONTEMPS, ARNA. The Story of George Washington Carver. Grosset & Dunlap, 1954. $1.95; Harper & Row paper $.72 (C)
> A moving portrait and unsentimental biography of a great scientist, this book should prove valuable for independent reading as well as for character-building and development of an understanding of minority groups.
> **I-UE**

GOLDIN, AUGUSTA. Straight Hair, Curly Hair. Crowell-Collier, 1966. $3.25

> Answers to questions children ask about their hair. The simple text tells how it grows, why hair is straight or curly, and how hair serves many beautiful purposes.
> **LE**

MANBER, DAVID. Wizard of Tuskegee. Crowell-Collier, 1967. $2.95 (LJ)

> Slightly more difficult reading than the biographies by Arna Bontemps, Florence Means, and Anne Terry White. The contributions that Carver made to space-age synthetics are emphasized.
> **I-UE**

RIPLEY, SHELDON N. Matthew Henson: Arctic Hero. Houghton Mifflin, 1966. $2.20 (ES)

> A biography of the man who accompanied and assisted Peary in the Arctic exploration. The book covers much of Henson's early life and ends at the time of his death. The story stresses man's determination to succeed by the merits of his own abilities and by dedicated service. For slower readers.
> **I-UE**

SHOWERS, PAUL. Your Skin and Mine. (Let's-Read-and-Find-Out Science Book). Thomas Y. Crowell, 1965. $3.25 (B)

> A little science book that can teach an important lesson in race relations.
> **LE**

STERNE, EMMA G. Blood Brothers: Four Men of Science. Alfred A. Knopf, 1959. $3.00 (HB)

> Four men famous for work in blood and heart research are treated in this collective biography. One of the four is Dr. Charles Drew, Negro, whose research in the use of blood

plasma won him recognition and the gratitude of many people. Easy supplementary reading.
I-UE

STEVENSON, AUGUSTA. George Carver: Boy Scientist. Bobbs-Merrill, 1944. $2.50 (C)
A biography in story form, dealing mainly with the early years of the great Negro scientist.
I-UE

Secondary

ANGELL, PAULINE. To the Top of the World: The Story of Peary and Henson. Rand McNally, 1964. $4.50 (LJ)
Controversy has long accompanied discussion of Henson's role in the Peary expedition, and the author has drawn upon authentic records to establish the importance of his contribution to the discovery of the North Pole.
See also Miller, Floyd, **Ahdoolo!**, page 42.
JH-SH

GRAHAM, SHIRLEY. Your Most Humble Servant: The Story of Benjamin Banneker. Julian Messner, 1949. $3.34 (B)
Inventor, astronomer, assistant to L'Enfant in the planning of the city of Washington, D. C.
JH-SH

HOLT, RACKHAM. George Washington Carver: An American Biography. Doubleday, 1942. $4.95; Abingdon paper $1.75 (SH)
A definitive treatment of the Negro teacher whose genius for extracting the secrets of nature to create useful products made him perhaps the most famous Negro of his time.
JH-SH

MILLER, FLOYD. Ahdoolo! E. P. Dutton, 1963. $4.50
A biography of Matthew Henson, who accompanied Admiral Robert E. Peary on his trip to the Arctic and was the first Negro to reach the North Pole.
JH-SH

SOCIAL SCIENCE

CIVIL RIGHTS

Secondary

BELFRAGE, SALLY. Freedom Summer. Viking Press, 1965. $5.00; Fawcett paper $.75 (SH)
A young white girl tells of her experiences as a SNCC worker with the 1964 Summer Project in Greenwood, Mississippi.
JH-SH

BENNETT, LERONE. What Manner of Man? Johnson, 1964. $4.95; Simon & Schuster paper $1.00 (SH)
A biography of civil rights leader Martin Luther King, Jr.
JH-SH

BERMAN, DANIEL M. A Bill Becomes A Law: The Civil Rights Act of 1960. Macmillan, 1966. Paper $1.95 (C)
The legislative history of the 1960 Civil Rights Act.
JH-SH

BLAIR, LEWIS H. A Southern Prophecy. Edited by C. Vann Woodward. Little, Brown, 1964. $5.00; paper $1.95 (LJ)
A recent edition of a book written one hundred years ago by a native-born Southerner who argued for Negro equality as the only means by which the South could compete with other regions of the nation. Although the author later repudiated his own arguments, his position can serve as an area for a discussion of civil rights for all citizens.
SH

BOYLE, SARAH PATTON. Desegregated Heart: A Virginian's Stand in Time of Transition. William Morrow, 1962. $5.00; paper $1.95 (LJ)
A personal narrative by a white woman of aristocratic back-

ground from Virginia who took up the cause of desegregation in her community and thereby became a controversial
figure.
SH

**BREETVELD, JIM. Getting to Know the Human Rights Com-
mission.** Coward-McCann, 1961. $2.50
Brief, illustrated history of the United Nations Commission
for Human Rights, which describes its functions in story
form and includes the full text of the Universal Declaration
of Human Rights. Important to the history of Negroes as it
represents the consensus of the members of the United Nations.
JH-SH

**BRINK, WILLIAM, and HARRIS, LOUIS. The Negro Revolu-
tion in America.** Simon & Schuster, 1964. $4.50; paper $1.45 (SH)
The subtitle—"What Negroes want; why and how they are
fighting; whom they support; what whites think of them and
their demands; based on a nationwide survey by **Newsweek**
magazine"—explains this opinion poll.
SH

**BRODERICK, FRANCIS L. W. E. B. DuBois: Negro Leader in
a Time of Crisis.** Stanford University Press, 1959. $6.75; paper
$2.95 (B)
A study of the famous and controversial Negro leader. Able
and mature high school seniors could use this as supplementary material for discussions of America in the twentieth
century, as well as for American history since the Civil War.
SH

**CLAYTON, EDWARD. Martin Luther King: The Peaceful
Warrior.** Prentice-Hall, 1964. $3.50
A short, romantic account of the Negro who believed in the
"peaceful revolution."
JH

CLEAVER, ELDRIDGE. Soul On Ice. McGraw-Hill, 1968. $5.95 (LJ)

In this collection of essays, Cleaver offers an analysis of American society that cuts away what he feels are the myths that have cloaked our motives at home and abroad.

SH

CLEMONS, LULAMAE, et al. The American Negro. McGraw-Hill, 1965. $1.48

This is the first title in the publisher's series, "Americans All," which treats the various ethnic and racial minorities in the United States. A wealth of information and excellent photographs are included. Could be used in sets for maximum classroom use in junior and senior high school.

JH-SH

CONOT, ROBERT. Rivers of Blood, Years of Darkness. William Morrow, 1968. $6.95

A superbly organized and readable history of the 1965 Watts riot.

SH

CRUSE, HAROLD. The Crisis of the Negro Intellectual. William Morrow, 1967. $8.95 (LJ)

A comprehensive, ideological examination of Negro intellectual development in America from the 1920's to the present.

SH

DANIEL, BRADFORD (editor). Black, White, and Gray: 21 Points of View on the Race Question. Sheed & Ward, 1964. $5.95 (LJ)

Governors Faubus and Connally, Martin Luther King, Jr., Harry Golden, and James Baldwin are among a varied group of contributors who present their ideas on the race question in the United States.

SH

DORMAN, MICHAEL. We Shall Overcome. Dial, 1964. $4.95 (LJ)

A trained and responsible journalist presents eyewitness accounts of the chief events in the battle for civil rights in the South in 1962 and 1963.

SH

EVERS, MRS. MEDGAR. For Us, The Living. Doubleday, 1968. $5.95

A significant story of the Negro revolution by the widow of a slain NAACP leader.

SH

FARMER, JAMES. Freedom—When? Random House, 1966. $4.95 (LJ)

A founder of the Congress of Racial Equality and its national director until 1966 gives a picture of the roles the various civil rights organizations play in the fight for freedom—with emphasis on the work of CORE.

SH

FRIEDMAN, LEON (editor). **Southern Justice.** Pantheon Books, 1965. $5.95; Meridian paper $2.45 (B)

Nineteen lawyers relate "how the law operates in regards to civil rights in the South."

SH

GOLDMAN, PETER. Civil Rights: Challenge of the Fourteenth Amendment. Coward-McCann, 1965. $2.60 (CCB)

High school government and history classes, including junior high classes studying current events, will find this helpful. Could also serve as an introduction to a serious study of the constitutional amendments resulting from the Civil War.

JH-SH

GRIGG, CHARLES. See Killian, Lewis M., page 49.

HANDLIN, OSCAR. Fire-bell in the Night. Little, Brown, 1964. $3.75; Beacon Press, 1965. Paper $.95 (SH)
The author examines the developments in civil rights during the last ten years and suggests what the results could be if Americans should fail to heed the fire-bell's call for racial equality.
SH

HARRIS, JANET. Long Freedom Road. McGraw-Hill, 1967. $3.95
The dramatic history of the civil rights movement.
JH-SH

HARRIS, LOUIS. See Brink, William, page 44.

HAYDEN, THOMAS. Rebellion in Newark. Random House, 1968. $3.95; paper $1.65.
The author, with four years of experience as a community organizer in the Newark Negro ghetto, draws on eyewitness and participant testimony concerning the Newark riot, July 12-17, 1967.
SH

HEDGEMAN, ANNA ARNOLD. The Trumpet Sounds: A Memoir of Negro Leadership. Holt, Rinehart & Winston, 1964. $4.95 (LJ)
A Negro leader tells of her experiences with segregation and her part in the fight for the rights of Negroes from 1922 until the March on Washington in 1963.
SH

HENTOFF, NAT. The New Equality. Viking Press, 1964. $4.95; paper $1.45 (LJ)

A commentary on Negro-white relations by the well-known jazz writer. He analyzes the widening differences between the "moderate" and the Negro "activist" and points up the importance of the federal government in using its powers to aid in the war on poverty and for better education and employment.
SH

HOLT, LEN. Summer That Didn't End. William Morrow, 1965. $5.00 (LJ)

Descriptions of events in Mississippi in the summer of 1964, written while the author was engaged actively in the civil rights movement. Appendices list documents supporting the author's views. For senior high school, American history, and American government classes. Average reading ability.
SH

HUGHES, LANGSTON. Fight for Freedom: The Story of the NAACP. W. W. Norton, 1962. $4.95 (B)

A distinguished Negro's account of the history of the National Association for the Advancement of Colored People includes legal victories as well as sketches of some of the leaders who have helped the movement along.
SH

HUIE, WILLIAM B. Three Lives for Mississippi. Trident Press, 1965. $4.95 (NYT)

A Southern writer gives the closest thing to an explanation we are likely to have for the disappearance of the three civil rights workers, Goodman, Chaney, and Schwerner.
SH

IANNIELLO, LYNNE (editor). Milestones Along the March: Twelve Historic Civil Rights Documents—from World War II to Selma. Frederick A. Praeger, 1966. $3.95 (C)

These documents begin with President Roosevelt's orders establishing the wartime F.E.P.C. and end with President Johnson's "We Shall Overcome" speech to Congress, March 1965. These documents, useful in themselves, point up the distance between words and deeds. For the advanced student.
SH

KILLIAN, LEWIS M., and GRIGG, CHARLES. Racial Crisis in America: Leadership in Conflict. Prentice-Hall, 1964. $4.50; paper $1.95 (NYT)
The thesis of this work is that, although token advances have been made, the real causes underlying inequality still exist. Points up the need for new approaches.
SH

KING, MARTIN LUTHER, JR. Stride Toward Freedom. Harper & Row, 1958. $4.95; paper $.65 (B)
An account of the Negro boycott of jim crow bus lines in Montgomery, Alabama.
SH

———. **Why We Can't Wait.** Harper & Row, 1964. $3.50; New American Library paper $.60 (HB)
In this eloquent description of the Birmingham demonstration and the March on Washington, the author strikes out against racial discrimination and gradualism.
SH

KUNSTLER, WILLIAM M. Deep in My Heart. William Morrow, 1966. $4.95 (LJ)
A civil rights lawyer, who has represented the causes of Martin Luther King, Jr., Dick Gregory, and others, gives his viewpoints on the "revolution."
SH

LEWIS, ANTHONY, and the NEW YORK TIMES. Portrait of a Decade: The Second American Revolution. Random House, 1964. $6.95 (LJ)

> Some of the material in this book is covered in Dorman's We Shall Overcome. However, Lewis covers a decade and skims over much that is detailed in the Dorman book. The two books could be used together; they supplement each other. Recommended for use in advanced American history and contemporary American problems.
>
> SH

LINCOLN, C. ERIC. My Face is Black. Beacon Press, 1964. $3.50

> A Methodist minister and professor relates the historical development of the Negro protest and points up black nationalism as a symbol of the new mood among some Negro Americans.
>
> SH

————. **Sounds of the Struggle: Persons and Perspectives in Civil Rights.** William Morrow, 1967. $5.00; Apollo paper $1.95 (LJ)

> Eighteen expressive articles, all but one previously published elsewhere.
>
> SH

LUBELL, SAMUEL. White and Black: Test of a Nation. 2nd ed. Harper & Row, 1964. $4.95; paper $1.60 (LJ)

> A political reporter and analyst reviews America's handling of the racial conflict during the one hundred years since Emancipation.
>
> SH

MELTZER, MILTON. Thaddeus Stevens and the Fight for Negro Rights. Thomas Y. Crowell, 1967. $4.50 (LJ)

> The documentary style is enlivened by questions from leading political figures of Stevens' day, and the work is supported by a good bibliography and an adequate index.
>
> JH-SH

MENDELSON, WALLACE. Discrimination. Prentice-Hall, 1962. Paper $1.95

> Summary of the reports of the U. S. Commission on Civil Rights regarding voting, education, employment, housing, and justice.
>
> **SH**

MEREDITH, JAMES. Three Years in Mississippi. Indiana University Press, 1966. $5.95 (LJ)

> The author tells of his days at an all-Negro college in Jackson, Mississippi, and explains his role at "Ole Miss."
>
> **SH**

MIERS, EARL S. Freedom. Grosset & Dunlap, 1965. $4.95 (NYT)

> Documentary photographs, engravings, paintings, and the text describe the struggle for American freedoms. Three of the struggles are related to the rights of Negroes.
>
> **JH**

MILLER, LOREN. The Petitioners: Story of the Supreme Court of the United States and the Negro. Pantheon Books, 1966. $8.95; Meridian paper $2.95 (C)

> A well-written history of the U. S. Supreme Court and its decisions relating to Negroes and their rights both as slaves and as freedmen between 1789 and 1965.
>
> **SH**

MITCHELL, GLENFORD E., and PEACE, WILLIAM (editors). Angry Black South. Citadel Press, 1962. $1.45

> Southern Negroes write about the present.
>
> **SH**

MORGAN, CHARLES. Time to Speak. Harper & Row, 1964. $3.95 (HB)

> After the episode of the church-burning in Birmingham, a young white Southern lawyer denounces the apathy and brutality of some of his fellow Alabamans.
>
> **SH**

NEW YORK TIMES. See Lewis, Anthony, page 50.

PARSONS, TALCOTT (editor). **The Negro American.** Houghton Mifflin, 1966. $9.50; Beacon paper $3.95 (LJ)
> Under the auspices of the American Academy of Arts and Sciences, civil rights leaders in the fields of history, economics, psychology, and sociology have written thirty essays on racial problems and their effect on American democracy.
> **SH**

PEACE, WILLIAM. See Mitchell, Glenford E., page 51.

PECK, JAMES. Freedom Ride. Simon & Schuster, 1962. $3.50 (LJ)
> A history of the Freedom Rides in 1947–1962 by one of the leading white participants. Firsthand accounts of jail-ins and sit-ins.
> **JH-SH**

PROUDFOOT, M. Diary of a Sit-in. University of North Carolina Press, 1962. $5.00; paper $1.95 (LJ)
> An account by one of the nonviolent sit-ins who helped to desegregate many of the Knoxville, Tennessee, lunch counters during June and July, 1960.
> **SH**

Report of the National Advisory Commission on Civil Disorders. Bantam Books, 1968. $1.25
> Explanations of the causes and remedies of the racial violence in America's cities, as reported by the Presidential Commission.
> **JH-SH**

ROCHE, JOHN P. The Quest for the Dream. Macmillan, 1963. $5.95
> Subtitled "The Development of Civil Rights and Human Relations in Modern America (since 1900)."
> **SH**

ROSE, ARNOLD M. (editor). **Assuring Freedom to the Free: A Century of Emancipation in the USA.** Wayne State University Press, 1964. $6.95 (LJ)

Papers presented at Wayne State University during 1963 at the 100th anniversary celebration of the Emancipation Proclamation. Topics of a general nature include jobs, housing, Black Muslims, and the law. Useful for term papers on subjects of Negroes in a changing society.

SH

SCHECTER, BETTY. Peaceable Revolution. Houghton Mifflin, 1964. $3.75 (ES)

The story of nonviolence as a philosophy of resistance, and Thoreau's and Ghandi's influence on the freedom movement of today.

JH-SH

SILBERMAN, CHARLES E. Crisis in Black and White. Random House, 1964. $5.95; paper $1.95 (LJ)

The author makes a plea for restoring to Negroes the dignity, initiative, and ambition of which their fellow Americans have traditionally deprived them.

SH

SMITH, LILLIAN E. Our Faces: Our Words. W. W. Norton, 1964. $3.75; paper $1.95 (LJ)

A noted novelist skillfully portrays the Civil Rights movement in a series of monologues and photographs.

JH-SH

STERLING, DOROTHY. Tear Down the Walls: A History of the American Civil Rights Movement. Doubleday, 1968. $4.95 (NYT)

Covers in a readable style the civil rights movement in the United States.

JH-SH

STERNE, EMMA G. I Have A Dream. Alfred A. Knopf, 1965. $3.95 (LJ)

> Included are biographies of Marian Anderson, A. Phillip Randolph, Captain Hugh Mulzac, Thurgood Marshall, Rosa Lee Parks, Daisy Bates, James Farmer, Fred Shuttleworth, and John Lewis.
> JH-SH

STONE, CHUCK. Tell It Like It Is. Trident Press, 1968 $4.95 (LJ)

> A Negro author tells about race relations in America through a collection of essays.
> SH

SUTHERLAND, ELIZABETH (editor). Letters from Mississippi. McGraw-Hill, 1965. $5.95; New American Library paper $.75 (LJ)

> In the summer of 1964, many white volunteers worked with Negroes in Mississippi. This is a collection of their letters written to families and friends.
> SH

VON HOFFMAN, NICHOLAS. Mississippi Notebook. David White, 1964. $4.50 (LJ)

> A firsthand report—dispassionate but sympathetic—of student involvement in civil rights activities during the eventful summer of 1964. High school students reading this and similar books may be led to ponder the meaning of courage and patriotism, as well as the meaning of fear.
> SH

WELTNER, CHARLES L. Southerner. J. B. Lippincott, 1966. $3.95 (LJ)

> Written by a former Southern congressman (Georgia), this book tells of the problems of the South and admits both that Negroes are also Southerners, and that they should have the same rights as white men.
> SH

WESTIN, ALAN F. (editor). **Freedom Now! The Civil Rights Struggle in America.** Basic Books, 1964. $6.95 (LJ)

> An anthology of fifty-one brief articles on "the moral dimensions of the civil rights struggle." A look at the management and methods of the struggle includes a wide range of opinions. Among the contributors are Martin Luther King, Jr., James Peck, and James Baldwin.
> **JH-SH**

WISH, HARVEY (editor). **The Negro Since Emancipation.** Prentice-Hall, 1964. $4.95; paper $1.95

> A comprehensive survey, in point of time, which includes selections by Frederick Douglass, Booker T. Washington, James Weldon Johnson, Carter G. Woodson, Richard Wright, Ralph Bunche, Martin Luther King, Jr., and others.
> **JH-SH**

WRIGHT, NATHAN, JR. Black Power and Urban Unrest. Hawthorn Books, 1967. $4.50; paper $1.95 (LJ)

> An analysis of the meaning and goals of Black Power by a Negro educator and executive director of the Department of Urban Work of the Episcopal Diocese of Newark, N.J.
> **SH**

ZINN, HOWARD. SNCC: The New Abolitionists. Beacon Press, 1964. $4.95; paper $1.75 (LJ)

> While a professor at Spelman College, Atlanta, Georgia, Zinn was advisor to the Student Non-Violent Coordinating Committee. He gives an account here of the movement from its beginning in 1960.
> **SH**

CUSTOMS AND FOLKLORE

Elementary

COURLANDER, HAROLD. Terrapin's Pot of Sense. Holt, Rinehart & Winston, 1957. $3.27 (C)

> A book of folk tales for children.
> **LE**

FELTON, HAROLD. John Henry and His Hammer. Alfred A. Knopf, 1950. $3.29 (C)

A retelling of the folk tales about John Henry, the giant Negro superman who worked on the railroads and told about his work in songs.

I-UE

KEATS, EZRA J. John Henry: American Legend. Pantheon Books, 1965. $3.50 (ES)

A well-illustrated story for children of all elementary levels.

LE

ROLLINS, CHARLEMAE H. Christmas Gif'. Follett, 1963. $4.95 (ES)

Southern Negroes over the years have played the game of Christmas Gif', a simple exchange of greetings at Christmastime. The first person to call out the phrase receives a small gift. In this collection of stories, poems, and favorite scriptures, the compiler has drawn upon traditional sources to provide an enjoyable look at the celebration of Christmas by Negroes. The material covers all age levels and reading ranges from easy to fairly difficult.

UE

WHITING, HELEN ADELE. Negro Folk-Tales. Associated Publishers, 1967. $1.40

Designed primarily for primary grade pupils, this book will cultivate a greater appreciation of Negro culture in children of all races.

LE-I

Secondary

BONTEMPS, ARNA. See Hughes, Langston, page 57.

DORSON, RICHARD M. American Negro Folktales. Fawcett (n.d.) $.75

Selected tales suitable for retelling in the classroom.

JH-SH

FELTON, HAROLD. John Henry and His Hammer.
See page 56.

HUGHES, LANGSTON, and BONTEMPS, ARNA (editors). Book of Negro Folklore. Dodd, Mead, 1958. $7.00 (B)

An anthology of Negro folk materials—songs, rhymes, games, spirituals, sermons, prayers, tales, street cries, and prose selections. Much of the material is in dialect and will be difficult to use, but the book is valuable for its inclusiveness and for the background information contained in the introductions to the various sections. Younger pupils may need teacher interpretation, but senior high readers should find the material useful.

JH-SH

HURSTON, ZORA NEALE. Mules and Men. J. B. Lippincott, 1935. $3.00 (B)

The first part of this book contains a collection of Negro folk tales; the second part describes modern voodoo practices.

SH

ROLLINS, CHARLEMAE H. Christmas Gif'.
See page 56.

EDUCATION

Elementary

PATTERSON, LILLIE. Booker T. Washington: Leader of His People. Garrard, 1962. $2.19

The author, a graduate of Hampton Institute, is proud of its most distinguished graduate, Booker T. Washington, and tells his story simply and with dignity.

I

STERNE, EMMA G. Mary McLeod Bethune. Alfred A. Knopf, 1957. $3.79 (ES)

> An inspiring story of the daughter of ex-slaves who rose from the depths of poverty to found a school and became an advisor to a President of the United States and bearer of the honorary title of First Lady of the Negro Race. Other good biographies of Mrs. Bethune are the following:
>
> **HOLT, RACKHAM. Mary McLeod Bethune.**
> **PEARE, C. O. Mary McLeod Bethune.**
> **I-UE**

STEVENSON, AUGUSTA. Booker T. Washington: Ambitious Boy. Bobbs-Merrill, 1950. $2.50 (C)

> The author tells the story of the childhood years of the slave boy who became founder and leader of Tuskegee Institute.
> **I**

Secondary

ANDERSON, MARGARET. The Children of the South. Farrar, Straus, 1966. $4.95; Dell paper $1.95 (HB)

> A former teacher and guidance counselor notes the effects—educational, psychological, and social—that the Supreme Court decision of 1954 had on Negro and white children.
> **SH**

ASHMORE, HARRY S. The Negro and the Schools. University of North Carolina Press, 1954. $1.50 (B)

> A summary of the work of forty-five scholars on the condition of Negro schools in five communities in 1954, prior to the Supreme Court decision.
> **SH**

BATES, DAISY. Long Shadow of Little Rock. David McKay, 1962. $5.50 (SH)

> Personal account of a Negro leader and her part in the integration of a Little Rock school.
> **SH**

BULLOCK, HENRY ALLEN. A History of Negro Education in the South. Harvard University Press, 1968. $7.95 (LJ)
> A study of educational policy and the treatment of the Negro school as a social institution.
> SH

CARRUTH, ELLA K. She Wanted to Read: The Story of Mary McLeod Bethune. Abingdon, 1966. $2.25
> Young Mary Bethune wanted to learn and share her learning with others. In this easy-to-read book, the author outlines the many activities of Mrs. Bethune, from the founding of Bethune-Cookman College to the great accomplishments in her later life. For less able readers in junior high.
> JH

KOZOL, JONATHAN. Death at an Early Age. Houghton Mifflin, 1967. $4.95; Bantam paper $.95 (LJ)
> An account of the problems of schools in Boston's ghettos. Winner of the 1967 National Book Award.
> SH

LORD, WALTER. The Past That Would Not Die. Harper & Row, 1965. $4.95; Pocket Books $.75 (SH)
> The story of cause and effect in enrolling James Meredith in the University of Mississippi.
> SH

MUSE, BENJAMIN. Ten Years of Prelude. Viking Press, 1964. $5.00 (LJ)
> The impact made by the Supreme Court decision of May 17, 1954, on the unconstitutionality of segregated schools.
> SH

SILVER, JAMES W. Mississippi: The Closed Society. Harcourt, Brace & World, 1964. $5.75; paper $1.75 (LJ)
> The author, a professor at the University of Mississippi during the rioting that preceded James Meredith's enrollment,

discusses the "closed society" that made the violence inevitable.
SH

STERNE, EMMA G. Mary McLeod Bethune.
See page 58.

WASHINGTON, BOOKER T. Up From Slavery. Doubleday, 1933. $4.95; Dodd, $3.95; Dell paper $.45 (SH)
The autobiography of the Negro educator who was born into slavery and who stressed the importance of economic rather than social advancement.
JH-SH

HISTORY

Elementary

BONTEMPS, ARNA. The Story of the Negro. 3rd ed. Alfred A. Knopf, 1958. $3.95 (C, SH)
Told in a style of great simplicity, the story moves easily from the African background, through the beginnings of the slave trade, to the introduction of the system of slavery into the New World, and its subsequent effect upon Africans and Americans in particular, and the world in general.
UE

BONTEMPS, ARNA, and CONROY, JACK. Frederick Douglass: Slave-Fighter, Freeman. Alfred A. Knopf, 1959. $3.19 (ES)
A good biography of the great Negro abolitionist, an ex-slave, whose golden tongue and militant attitude moved enemies to rage and friends to exert energy on behalf of slaves and freedmen. Fifth and sixth grade readers and slow readers in junior high school will find this book of interest.
UE

CONROY, JACK. See Bontemps, Arna, page 60.

CUBAN, LARRY. The Negro in America. Scott, Foresman, 1964. Paper $1.80
> A timely collection of source materials that will be useful for collateral reading in both English and history classes.
> I-UE

DRISKO, CAROL, and TOPPIN, EDGAR A. The Unfinished March: The Negro in the United States, Reconstruction to World War I. Doubleday, 1967. $2.95; paper $1.45 (HB)
> An easy-to-read, factual, and sympathetic account of Negro history between the Civil War and World War I.
> UE

FROME, MICHAEL. Virginia. Coward-McCann, 1967. $3.64 (LJ)
> Describes how some 500 Virginia Negroes enlisted by the Old Dominion as soldiers, spies, sailors, and Chesapeake pilots earned fame for their courage.
> UE

HUGHES, LANGSTON. Famous American Negroes. Dodd, Mead, 1954. $3.50 (ES)
> Seventeen biographies of Negro men and women who have achieved success in various fields. The figures in this book are better known than those included in **Famous Negro Heroes of America** by the same author. Included in this reference are an excellent introduction, an index, and photographs.
> I-UE

———. **Famous Negro Heroes of America.** Dodd, Mead, 1958. $3.50 (ES)
> A companion volume to **Famous American Negroes.** Included are biographies of sixteen less well-known figures who have achieved success in various fields of American life.
> I-UE

HUGHES, LANGSTON, and MELTZER, MILTON. A Pictorial History of the Negro in America. Crown, 1963. $5.95 (SH, C)
>Glimpses of Negro Americans through pictures and text.

JOHNSTON, JOHANNA. Together in America. Dodd, Mead, 1965. $3.50 (LJ)
>An attempt to show that people of both European and African descent have contributed to America's discovery, growth, and strength.
>UE

LEVENSON, DOROTHY. The First Book of the Civil War. Franklin Watts, 1968. $2.65 (LJ)
>This book can be read by many children below fifth grade. Among the topics discussed are economic factors that contributed to Northern strength, tension between the military and the press, contributions of Negroes to the war effort, information about uniforms and weapons, hospital conditions, and the ambivalent nature of the slavery issue.
>I-UE

MEIER, AUGUST. See Meltzer, Milton, page 62.

MELTZER, MILTON. See Hughes, Langston, page 62.

MELTZER, MILTON, and MEIER, AUGUST. Time of Trial, Time of Hope. Doubleday, 1966. $2.95; paper $1.45 (ES)
>An account of the social and economic conditions of the Negro in America between World War I and World War II.
>UE

PATTERSON, LILLIE. Frederick Douglass: Freedom Fighter. Garrard, 1965. $2.19 (ES)
>Similar in format and presentation to other volumes in the "Discovery" Book Series, this simple biography includes

brief facts about the life of Frederick Douglass. It covers his years of slavery, his escape, his activities as a spokesman for Negroes, and his death in 1895. This would be especially useful as easy reading material on minority groups.
LE-I

STERLING, DOROTHY. Captain of the Planter: The Story of Robert Smalls. Doubleday, 1958. $3.50 (HB)
The story of the ex-slave who became the first Negro commissioned as an officer in the Union Navy.
UE

————. **Forever Free: The Story of the Emancipation Proclamation.** Doubleday, 1963. $3.95 (ES)
A warmly told story tracing the events that led to the issuance of the Proclamation.
UE

STRATTON, MADELINE ROBINSON. Negroes Who Helped Build America. Ginn, 1965. $3.00 (B)
A collection of fourteen biographies of Robert Abbott, Marian Anderson, Mary M. Bethune, Ralph Bunche, B. O. Davis, Frederick Douglass, Charles Drew, W. E. B. DuBois, Percy Julian, Martin Luther King, Jr., Jackie Robinson, Booker T. Washington, Daniel H. Williams, and Carter G. Woodson. There is no index but a bibliography is appended.
UE

TOPPIN, E. A. See Drisko, Carol, page 61.

YATES, ELIZABETH. Amos Fortune, Free Man. E. P. Dutton, 1950. $3.50 (HB)
Winner of the Newbery Award, this is the story of an obscure Negro who was born in Africa and became enslaved in America. Through arduous toil, he freed himself and several other slaves and became the benefactor of the small community of Jaffrey, New Hampshire, which still enjoys his legacy.
UE

YOUNG, MARGARET B. First Book of Negroes. Franklin
Watts, 1967. $2.65 (ES)
> History, biography, education, employment, and the contri-
> butions of American Negroes as well as the civil rights move-
> ment are covered in an account of Negroes' struggles and
> accomplishments from 1619 to the present.
> **UE**

Secondary

ADAMS, RUSSELL L. Great Negroes: Past and Present. 2nd ed.
by D. P. Ross. Afro-American, 1964. $5.95
> Pictures and text about Negroes—from African chieftains
> and warriors to present-day leaders in science, business,
> politics, religion, education, and the arts.
> **JH-SH**

APTHEKER, HERBERT. American Negro Slave Revolts. International, 1963. $2.25 (LJ)
> Some 250 Negro slave revolts are documented, but little
> mention of these uprisings has been included in the standard
> texts of American history. This account will change the
> image of Negroes as chattels, happy in their bondage, and
> will present a much more realistic picture of the slaves and
> the institution of slavery.
> **JH-SH**
———— **(editor). A Documentary History of the Negro People in
the United States.** 2 vols. Citadel Press, 1962. $2.75 each (SH)
> The first volume covers colonial times through the Civil
> War. Volume Two covers the Reconstruction period to the
> founding of the NAACP in 1910.
> **JH-SH**

BARDOLPH, RICHARD. The Negro Vanguard. Vintage, 1961.
Paper $1.85 (B)
> Biographies of outstanding Negroes from 1770 to the pres-
> ent, with an emphasis on their origins, their careers, and

their approach to white middle-class values, attitudes, and behavior.
SH

BENNETT, LERONE. Before the Mayflower. Johnson, 1962. $6.95; Penguin paper $2.45 (LJ)
The story of Negro Americans from the days of Africa to the sit-in generation of the 1960's.
JH-SH
————. **Black Power USA.** Johnson, 1967. $6.95 (LJ)
A readable and factual interpretation of Reconstruction, 1867-1877. Very useful for presenting an objective view of Negroes and this controversial period.
JH-SH

BERNARD, JACQUELINE. Journey Toward Freedom. W. W. Norton, 1967. $4.50 (NYT)
The story of Sojourner Truth, a former slave who preached for emancipation and women's rights.
JH-SH

BONTEMPS, ARNA. One Hundred Years of Negro Freedom. Dodd, Mead, 1961. $4.25; Morrow paper $1.95 (ES, JH, SH)
The lives and personalities of Negro leaders since the Emancipation Proclamation—from Senator Pinchback to Martin Luther King, Jr. Includes portraits of little-known men.
JH-SH
————. **The Story of the Negro.**
See page 60.

BONTEMPS, ARNA, and CONROY, JACK. Anyplace But Here. Hill and Wang, 1966. $5.95; paper $1.95 (SH)
This revision of **They Seek A City** (1945) deals with Negro migrations in the United States and gives brief biographies of outstanding Negroes from the seventeenth century to the

present day. The last part of the book deals with Negro na-
tionalism, Malcolm X, and the Watts riot.
JH-SH
————. **Frederick Douglass: Slave-Fighter, Freeman.**
See page 60.

BOTKIN, B. A. (editor). Lay My Burden Down. University of
Chicago Press, 1945. Paper $1.95 (SH)
> A collection of firsthand experiences as related by ex-slaves to
> members of the W.P.A. Writer's Project during the years of
> the Depression.
> **SH**

BRODERICK, FRANCIS. See Meier, August, page 72.

BUCKMASTER, HENRIETTA. Flight to Freedom. Thomas Y.
Crowell, 1958. $3.95 (HB)
> Dramatic story of the Underground Railroad, told through
> the lives of those—Negro and white—who participated in it.
> Her **Let My People Go** is another book on the same subject.
> **JH-SH**

BUTCHER, MARGARET. Negro in American Culture. Alfred A. Knopf, 1956. $5.95 (SH)
> Materials left by Alain Locke form the basis of this history
> of the role of Negroes in American society, their culture as
> slaves, as freemen, and as citizens.
> **SH**

COMMAGER, HENRY STEELE. Crusaders for Freedom.
Doubleday, 1962. $3.95 (HB)
> Inspiring biographies of Negroes and whites who fought for
> freedom of speech, religion, and emancipation.
> **JH-SH**

CONROY, JACK. See Bontemps, Arna, pages 60 and 65.

CRONON, E. DAVID. Black Moses: The Story of Marcus Garvey and the Universal Negro Improvement Association. University of Wisconsin Press, 1955. $6.00; paper $1.95 (B)

Black Moses is the first full-length, objective book about the Jamaica-born Negro Marcus Garvey, who three decades ago created a significant stir on the American scene.

SH

CUBAN, LARRY. The Negro in America.

See page 61.

DAVIDSON, BASIL. Black Mother: The Years of the African Slave Trade. Little, Brown, 1961. $6.95 (B)

The book is a good starting point for readers seriously interested in the history of slavery.

SH

DOBLER, LAVINIA, and TOPPIN, E. A. Pioneers and Patriots: The Lives of Six Negroes of the Revolutionary Era. Doubleday, 1965. $2.95; paper $1.45 (ES, JH)

Biographies of six Negroes who contributed to America's fight for independence and her growth as a nation. Each profile is brief and simply written. Included are Peter Salem, Jean Baptiste Pointe de Sable, Phillis Wheatley, Benjamin Banneker, Paul Cuffe, and John Chavis.

JH

DOUGLASS, FREDERICK. Life and Times of Frederick Douglass. Thomas Y. Crowell, 1966. $3.95; Macmillan paper $2.45 (ES)

An excellent background for the study of the present struggle for equality. Perhaps the story of Douglass' early days and the drama of his escape to freedom will prove more interesting than the internal conflicts within the abolitionist movement.

JH-SH

————. The Mind and Heart of Frederick Douglass: Excerpts from Speeches of the Great Negro Orator. Thomas Y. Crowell, 1968. $4.50 (LJ)

> This volume brings to students of Negro history fascinating speeches until now available only in the four-volume **Life and Writing of Frederick Douglass.**
> JH-SH

DRISKO, CAROL, and TOPPIN, EDGAR A.
> See page 61.

DURHAM, PHILIP, and JONES, E. L. Adventures of the Negro Cowboys. Dodd, Mead, 1965. $5.00 (C, SH)

> Of interest to those who study the Old West are these descriptive and vivid case histories of Negro cowboys who rode the ranges from Texas to Montana.
> JH-SH

EICHNER, ALFRED S. See Ginzberg, Eli, page 69.

FELTON, HAROLD W. Jim Beckwourth: Negro Mountain Man. Dodd, Mead, 1966. $3.50 (LJ)

> Drawing largely from the autobiography of Jim Beckwourth, now out of print, the author has recreated the life and adventures of that almost legendary Negro mountain man, who worked with some of the best known scouts and fur traders, such as Kit Carson and Jim Bridges.
> JH-SH

FISHEL, LESLIE H., and QUARLES, BENJAMIN. The Negro American: A Documentary History. William Morrow, 1968. $6.95 (LJ)

> Selected documents include newspaper articles, speeches, personal accounts, and other records that trace the history of the Negro from Africa to the March on Washington.
> SH

FRANKLIN, JOHN HOPE. Emancipation Proclamation. Doubleday, 1963. $3.50; paper $.95 (LJ)

> Well-researched account of the origin, circumstances, impact, and moral and humanitarian significance of the Emancipation Proclamation.
> **SH**

————. **From Slavery to Freedom: A History of American Negroes.** rev. ed. Alfred A. Knopf, 1967. $10.75 (B)

> This text provides a political, cultural, and social survey of Negroes "from slavery to freedom."
> **SH**

————. **Reconstruction After the Civil War.** University of Chicago Press, 1961. $5.00; paper $1.95 (B)

> A modern interpretation of the Reconstruction period. Less difficult to read than DuBois' **Black Reconstruction.**
> **SH**

FRAZIER, E. FRANKLIN. The Negro in the United States. rev. ed. Macmillan, 1957. $8.95 (JH, SH)

> A large amount of information on Negro Americans and the problems of their integration into American life is presented in this encyclopedic study.
> **JH-SH**

FROME, MICHAEL. Virginia.

> See page 61.

GINZBERG, ELI, and EICHNER, ALFRED S. The Troublesome Presence. Macmillan, 1964. $6.50 (SH)

> A readable survey of the period from 1619 to the present that discusses the impact of Negroes on America and of America on Negroes. It provides background for the present tensions and points up the cost to the nation of continuing to deny Negroes their rights.
> **SH**

GOLDSTON, ROBERT. The Negro Revolution. Macmillan, 1968. $4.95 (LJ)
> A sweeping picture of the whole of Negro history from ancient Africa to the present. Ideally suited for high school students because of the maturity of vocabulary and discussions included.
> JH-SH

GRAHAM, SHIRLEY. Jean Baptiste Pointe de Sable, Founder of Chicago. Julian Messner, 1953. $3.34 (LJ)
> The story of Pointe de Sable, explorer and trader, who founded the city of Chicago.
> JH-SH

HUGHES, LANGSTON. Famous American Negroes.
> See page 61.

HUGHES, LANGSTON, and MELTZER, MILTON. A Pictorial History of the Negro in America.
> See page 62.

JOHNSTON, JOHANNA. Special Bravery. Dodd, Mead, 1967. $3.50 (NYT)
> These stories, written in poetic prose, relate some of the achievements of fifteen Negro Americans and the hardships under which they achieved the citation for "special bravery."
> JH-SH
——. **Together in America.**
> See page 62.

JONES, E. L. See Durham, Philip, page 68.

KATZ, William L. (editor). Eyewitness: The Negro in American History. Pitman, 1967. $9.75 (NYT)
> Clearly written narratives of every period in our history, drawn from letters, army records, diaries, newspapers, and other primary sources.
> JH-SH

LEE, IRVIN H. Negro Medal of Honor Men. Dodd, Mead, 1967. $4.00 (CCB)

A history of Negro participation in American military history, with emphasis on the deeds of valor that merited the Medal of Honor.

JH-SH

LEE, ULYSSES. The Employment of Negro Troops. U.S. Government Printing Office, Washington, D.C., 1966. $7.75

This book takes a look at the Army's policy of "separate but equal," the troubles encountered, and the measures taken to solve the problems.

SH

LOGAN, RAYFORD. See Sterling, Philip, page 76.

McCARTHY, AGNES, and REDDICK, L. Worth Fighting For: A History of the Negro in the United States during the Civil War and Reconstruction. Doubleday, 1965. $2.95; paper $1.45 (B)

This book introduced a new historical series called "Zenith Books." Its purpose, as stated by the publisher, is to present the history of American minority groups and the story of their participation in the growth and development of the United States. Other titles in the "Zenith" series are: **A Glorious Age in Africa; Guide to African Past; Great Rulers of the African Past; Let Freedom Ring;** and **Pioneers and Patriots.**

McPHERSON, JAMES M. Marching Toward Freedom: The Negro in the Civil War 1861-1865. Alfred A. Knopf, 1968. $3.95 (NYT)

Vivid eyewitness accounts of how Negro spies, soldiers, nurses, cooks, etc., battled courageously for freedom.

JH-SH

————. **The Negro's Civil War.** Pantheon Books, 1965. $6.95; Vintage paper $1.95 (SH)

A study of the militant part Negroes played in the war for their emancipation. Brings together a wide variety of speeches, letters, articles, and official documents to disprove the common idea that Negroes were the passive recipients of freedom.

SH

————. **The Struggle for Equality: Abolitionists and the Negro in the Civil War and Reconstruction.** Princeton University Press, 1964. $10.00; paper $3.45 (SH)

An analysis of the role played by the abolitionists during and after the Civil War and their relationship to the Republican Party.

SH

MEIER, AUGUST, and BRODERICK, FRANCIS (editors). Negro Protest Thought in the Twentieth Century. (The American Heritage Series). Bobbs-Merrill, 1965. $7.50; paper $3.25 (LJ)

This report on the Negro protest movement from Booker T. Washington to today's CORE spells out the changes in Negro attitudes from accommodation to open rejection. It is essentially a presentation of actual speeches, documents, reports, and editorials.

JH-SH

MELTZER, MILTON (editor). In Their Own Words: A History of the American Negro. 3 vols. Thomas Y. Crowell, 1967. $4.95 each; paper $1.45 each (LJ)

A history of Negro Americans as told in their own words, taken from original sources. Recommended as a resource book for teachers and advanced upper-grade readers. See also: Botkin, B. A., **Lay My Burden Down,** and Aptheker, Herbert, **Documentary History of the Negro People in the United States.**

SH

MIERS, EARL SCHENCK. The Story of the American Negro. Grosset & Dunlap, 1965. $1.95 (LJ)

> Brief history of the American Negro, tracing his origins in Africa and highlighting his contribution to American history up to and including the Freedom March on Washington, August 28, 1963.
>
> JH

MORSBACK, MABEL. The Negro in American Life. Harcourt, Brace & World, 1967. $6.95 (CCB)

> An overview of Negro history, prefaced by brief chapters on African background and on the role of immigrants and minority groups in the New World. The material is chronologically arranged, with comments on the role of the Negro people or brief biographical sketches incorporated into general historical information.
>
> JH-SH

PAULI, HERTHA. Her Name was Sojourner Truth. Appleton-Century-Crofts, 1962. $4.95 (LJ)

> The biography of a former slave and abolitionist who spent her life fighting for the rights of Negroes.
>
> SH

PETRY, ANN. Harriet Tubman: Conductor on the Underground Railroad. Thomas Y. Crowell, 1955. $3.95 (HB)

> This is a biography of the famous Negro woman who has been called the "Moses" of her people. Indispensable to a study of the period preceding the Civil War and ideal for use with "courage themes." Other similar biographies: Dorothy Sterling, **Freedom Train;** Anne Parrish, **A Clouded Star** (fiction); and Hildegarde Swift, **Railroad to Freedom.**
>
> JH-SH

QUARLES, BENJAMIN. Lincoln and the Negro. Oxford University Press, 1962. $6.50 (LJ)

A definitive study of the changes in Lincoln's attitude toward Negroes and their change toward Lincoln as the Civil War progressed. This is an interesting study and could be the source for a heated and illuminating discussion in high school history and government classes. Compare with W. O. Douglas' **Mr. Lincoln and the Negroes,** Atheneum, 1963.

SH

————. **The Negro in the American Revolution.** University of North Carolina Press, 1961. $6.00; paper $1.95 (LJ)

A well-documented study of the roles Negro soldiers played in the Revolutionary War. The book also sheds light on British efforts to influence Negro soldiers, and makes mention of the help afforded the colonies by Haitian soldiers who were in sympathy with their cause.

SH

————. **The Negro in the Civil War.** Russell, 1953. $10.00 (B)

A general survey of the role of Negroes in the Civil War, and a description of their contributions in military and behind-the-lines activities.

SH

————. See Fishel, Leslie H., page 68.
————. See Sterling, Dorothy, page 76.

REDDICK, L. See McCarthy, Agnes, page 71.

REDDING, J. SAUNDERS. The Lonesome Road. Doubleday, 1958. $5.95; paper $1.45 (B)

A survey of the part played by Negroes in America as told through the biographies of twelve Negro leaders, from Daniel Payne to Thurgood Marshall.

JH-SH

————. **The Negro.** Potomac Books, 1967. $3.75 (NYT)

The author tells of the origins of Negro servitude and the trauma of Civil War and Reconstruction. In the final chapters, he outlines the present Negro Revolution and the hopes and problems it has created in a maturing democracy. **JH-SH**

ROLLINS, CHARLEMAE. They Showed the Way. Thomas Y. Crowell, 1964. $3.00 (HB)

A much-needed addition to the biography collection, these capsule studies of forty Negro Americans emphasize the overwhelming difficulties they overcame to achieve success. **JH-SH**

ROSE, W. L. Rehearsal for Reconstruction. Bobbs-Merrill, 1964. $6.50; Vintage paper $1.95 (NYT)

An important book for any study of the Reconstruction efforts to cope with the problems of the freedmen. **SH**

SPANGLER, EARL. The Negro in America. Lerner Publications, 1966. $3.95 (ES)

A well-written and interesting book that succeeds fairly well in shifting emphasis from the Negro per se to U.S. history. The format is good; illustrations are numerous and well placed. **SH**

STAMPP, KENNETH M. The Peculiar Institution. Alfred A. Knopf, 1956. $6.95; Vintage paper $1.95 (LJ)

Through unbiased re-examination of Negro slavery in the South, the author destroys many long-accepted myths and substitutes the results of long and thorough research. A very useful title on the period of Reconstruction is his **Era of Reconstruction.** Knopf, 1965. **SH**

STERLING, DOROTHY. Captain of the Planter: The Story of Robert Smalls.
See page 63.
———. **Forever Free: The Story of the Emancipation Proclamation.**
See page 63.

STERLING, DOROTHY, and QUARLES, BENJAMIN. Lift Every Voice. Doubleday, 1965. $2.95; paper $1.45 (CCB)
The biographies of four Negro leaders: Mary Church Terrell, W. E. B. DuBois, James Weldon Johnson, and Booker T. Washington.
JH

STERLING, PHILIP, and LOGAN, RAYFORD. Four Took Freedom. Doubleday, 1967. $2.95; paper $1.45 (HB)
The lives of Harriet Tubman, Frederick Douglass, Robert Smalls, and Blanche K. Bruce. The illustrations are by Charles White, the outstanding Negro artist.
JH-SH

STERNE, EMMA G. Long Black Schooner. Scholastic Paperback, 1953. $1.75 (LJ)
An exciting re-creation of an important event in the history of Negroes in the United States—probably the first case presented to the U.S. Supreme Court that directly involved black men and women. Useful in the study of the slave trade and the abolitionist movement in the nineteenth century.
JH-SH
———. **They Took Their Stand.** Macmillan, 1968. $4.50 (NYT)
Offers profiles of twelve Southern white defenders of Negro rights, from Angeline Grimke, the abolitionist, and John Fairfield, an underground railroad "conductor," to Robert Zellner, a SNCC field worker.
SH

SWIFT, HILDEGARDE H. North Star Shining.
See page 36.
———. **Railroad to Freedom.** Harcourt, Brace & World, 1932.
$3.95 (B)
An exciting, fictionalized account of Harriet Tubman's life
up to the end of the Civil War.
JH

TOPPIN, E. A. See Dobler, Lavinia, page 67.

**WADE, RICHARD C. Slavery in the Cities: The South, 1820-
1860.** Oxford University Press, 1964. $6.75 (NYT)
An examination of the urban experiences of slaves, based
on a study of a ring of Southern cities in the antebellum
period. This is a greatly neglected area in the study of
slavery in America and the author has opened up new areas
for discussion and research.
SH

WOODSON, CARTER G. The Negro in Our History. 10th rev.
ed. by Charles H. Wesley. Associated Publishers, 1962. $10.00 (B)
This is a work of general information about the Negro, of
special value to senior high school and college students, but
of interest to anyone seeking material on Negro life and
history.
SH
———. **Negro Makers of History.** Revised by Charles H. Wesley.
Associated Publishers, 1958. $4.50 (SH)
A chronology of Negro life and history for high school
as well as college students. The format is similar to that
of a textbook. Each chapter is followed by a page entitled
"Facts to be Kept in Mind" and "Hints and Questions."
JH-SH

YATES, ELIZABETH. Amos Fortune, Free Man.
See page 63.

POLITICS

Secondary

CLAYTON, EDWARD T. The Negro Politician. Johnson, 1960. $4.95 (LJ)

A factual survey of past and present Negroes in politics.
JH-SH

KUGELMASS, ALVIN. Ralph Bunche: Fighter for Peace. Julian Messner, 1962. $3.50 (SH)

A biography of Dr. Ralph Bunche, the first Negro to win the Nobel Peace Prize for his mediation of the conflict between the Arabs and Israelis in 1948. Unfortunately, there appears to be no other full-length biography of Dr. Bunche that provides a thoughtful study of so important a figure. For World History, especially the period since World War II. Easy reading for junior and senior high pupils.
JH-SH

MATTHEWS, DONALD R., and PROTHRO, J. W. Negroes and the New Southern Politics. Harcourt, Brace & World, 1966. $12.50 (LJ)

Analyses of what the vote has meant to Southern Negroes, why they have not voted to their full potential, and a prediction of the future of the Negro vote.
SH

MORROW, E. FREDERIC. Black Man in the White House. Coward-McCann, 1963. $5.95; McFadden paper $.60 (LJ)

Diary of the first Negro to serve on a Presidential staff in an executive capacity. The author gives his views on the Eisenhower Administration, the Republican Party, and civil rights.
SH

PROTHRO, J. W. See Matthews, Donald, page 78.

RECORD, WILSON. The Negro and the Communist Party.
University of North Carolina Press, 1951. Paper $3.50 (B)
> Kremlin tactics and the rights of Negro Americans: a review of how the "Party" tries to use this dilemma.
> **SH**

————. **Race and Radicalism: The NAACP and the Communist Party in Conflict.** Cornell University Press, 1964. $5.95; paper $1.95 (LJ)
> An account of the ways in which the Communists have attempted unsuccessfully to gain a foothold in the NAACP.
> **SH**

RACE RELATIONS

Secondary

ASHLEY MONTAGU, M. F. Idea of Race. University of Nebraska Press, 1965. $4.00 (C)
> The three lectures included in the book trace the history of the idea of racial differences, pose and refute racist arguments, and finally give scientific evidence to support the author's thesis. His concepts are presented logically and the language is understandable to the serious high school student. For contemporary American problems.
> **SH**

————. **Man's Most Dangerous Myth: The Fallacy of Race.**
World, 1964. $7.50; paper $2.65 (LJ)
> A popular but thorough treatment of the modern concept of race, including a full discussion of race as a far-reaching social problem. Classes in contemporary American problems or modern social issues would find this book very useful; it could be used for teacher background.
> **SH**

BARUCH, DOROTHY. Glass House of Prejudice. William Morrow, 1946. $4.00 (B)

The causes and effects of prejudice are presented by a competent author who also offers practical suggestions that could effect changes in behavior.

SH

BOWEN, DAVID. The Struggle Within: Race Relations in the United States. W. W. Norton, 1965. $3.50 (SH)

An excellent introduction and general survey that presents facts surrounding the problems of race relations in this country from slavery to the present day.

SH

BOYLE, SARAH PATTON. For Human Beings Only. Seabury, 1964. $1.25

A superb guide for dealing with the labyrinth of feelings and emotions in Negro-white encounters.

SH

BRINK, WILLIAM, and HARRIS, LOUIS. Black and White: A Study of U.S. Racial Attitudes Today. Simon & Schuster, 1967. $5.95; paper $1.95 (LJ)

This is an expanded version of the **Newsweek** study made in 1966.

JH-SH

BROOM, LEONARD, and GLENN, N. D. Transformation of the Negro American. Harper & Row, 1965. $5.75; paper $1.75

A summary discussion of the way of life of Negroes with regard to nationalization, gradualism, education, business, and integration.

SH

BROWN, FRANCIS J., and ROUCEK, J. S. One America: The History, Contributions and Present Problems of our Racial and National Minorities. 3rd ed. Prentice-Hall, 1952. $7.35
> Useful, basic compendium of information about America's foreign-born and native ethnic population.
> **SH**

CLARK, KENNETH B. Dark Ghetto: Dilemmas of Social Power. Harper & Row, 1965. $5.95; paper $1.75 (SH)
> A penetrating analysis of the Negro power structure, the psychology of the ghetto, and the effectiveness and weaknesses of the techniques that currently implement the struggle for civil rights. Classes in government and economics will find this a good source for discussion material on current problems facing the American people. For advanced students.
> **SH**

GLENN, N. D. See Broom, Leonard, page 80.

GREGORY, DICK. The Shadow That Scares Me. Doubleday, 1968. $4.50 (LJ)
> Provocative and stimulating insights into what is and what is not true of our society.
> **JH-SH**

HANDLIN, OSCAR. Race and Nationality in American Life. Little, Brown, 1957. $4.95; Doubleday paper $1.25 (B)
> This analysis of the origins and bases for racial bigotry in the United States attacks the myth of race and scrutinizes the emotional-psychological insecurities of Americans.
> **SH**

HARRIS, LOUIS. See Brink, William, page 80.

KILLENS, JOHN OLIVER. Black Man's Burden. Trident Press, 1966. $3.95 (LJ)

This book analyzes the image white men have created of Negroes—the happy Negro slaves—and challenges both Negro and white Americans to work for a truly equal society.
SH

KING, MARTIN LUTHER, JR. Strength to Love. Harper & Row, 1963. $3.50; Pocket Books paper $.50 (LJ)

A collection of seventeen sermons by the well-known advocate of nonviolent action.
JH-SH

LOMAX, LOUIS E. Negro Revolt. Harper & Row, 1962. $4.50; New American Library paper $.95 (SH)

A brief history of race relations from the American Revolution to the present. Points out differences in Negro militancy among members of the Urban League, CORE, SNCC, SCLC, NAACP, and the Black Muslims.
JH-SH

MARROW, ALFRED J. Changing Patterns of Prejudice. Chilton, 1962. $7.50 (LJ)

Detailed analysis of a pressing social problem, by the former chairman of New York City's Commission on Intergroup Relations. For advanced senior high pupils.
SH

MASON, PHILIP. Common Sense About Race. (Common Sense Series). Macmillan, 1961. $2.95; Doubleday paper $1.25 (B)

A British expert on race relations analyzes the causes and costs of prejudice, scientifically disputes the racial superiority myth, and suggests actions for easing racial tensions.
SH

POWDERMAKER, HORTENSE. Probing Our Prejudices: A Unit for High School Students. Harper & Row. 1944. $2.50 (B)
A study of the nature, origin, and effect of prejudice that provides some basic understanding. Teachers may need to update some of this material in order to use it effectively with senior high school pupils.
JH-SH

ROUCEK, J. S. See Brown, Francis J., page 81.

SAMS, JESSE B. White Mother. McGraw-Hill, 1957. $4.50 (B)
Set in Florida, this is an inspiring narrative of two little Negro girls rescued from an impoverished, hopeless, and loveless life by a compassionate white woman whom they come to love as their mother.
JH-SH

WHITE, WILLIAM LINDSAY. Lost Boundaries. Harcourt, Brace & World, 1948. $2.75 (HB)
The true story of a Negro family that was "passing" for white and its effects upon the eldest child when he discovered he was a Negro.
JH-SH

YOUNG, WHITNEY M., JR., To Be Equal. McGraw-Hill, 1964. $5.00; paper $1.95 (LJ)
The Executive Director of the Urban League discusses the reasons for Negro demands and suggests extensive programs in the areas of employment, education, housing, and health for all citizens—Negro and white.
SH

SOCIAL CONDITIONS AND SITUATIONS

Secondary

BARTH, ERNEST A. See Northwood, L. K., page 87.

BOOKER, SIMEON. Black Man's America. Prentice-Hall, 1964. $4.95 (LJ)

A Negro reporter tells in journalistic style what it was like to be a White House reporter during the Eisenhower-Nixon adminstration.

SH

BROWN, CLAUDE. Manchild in the Promised Land. Macmillan, 1965. $5.95; New American Library paper $.95 (LJ)

All the ugliness and injustice of the Harlem ghetto during the years 1940 to 1950 are detailed in this autobiography.

SH

CAYTON, HORACE R. See Drake, St. Clair, page 84.

COHEN, JERRY, and MURPHY, W. S. Burn, Baby, Burn! E. P. Dutton, 1966. $5.95; Avon paper $.75 (LJ)

This description of the Watts riots of August 1965 by two reporters of the **Los Angeles Times** examines events leading up to the riots, the results, and the outlook for the future.

SH

DAVIE, MAURICE R. Negroes in American Society. McGraw-Hill, 1949. $7.50 (B)

A comprehensive textbook that takes in all aspects of Negro American life.

SH

DRAKE, ST. CLAIR, and CAYTON, HORACE R. Black Metropolis: A Study of Negro Life in a Northern City. Harper & Row, 2 vols., 1963. Paper $2.75 each (B)

A classic study that deals with Negroes in the city of Chicago.

SH

DUNBAR, ERNEST. The Black Expatriates: A Study of American Negroes in Exile. E. P. Dutton, 1968. $4.95 (LJ)
>Dunbar, a senior editor of Look Magazine, interviews sixteen American Negroes who, for various reasons, decided to leave America and live elsewhere.
SH

ESSIEN-UDOM, E. Black Nationalism: A Search for an Identity in America. University of Chicago Press, 1963. $7.50; Dell paper $.75 (B)
>Nigerian-born Essien-Udom believes that the tragedy of Negro Americans is that they have rejected their origins. He discusses black nationalism in the United States, taking a sympathetic view of Black Muslims.
SH

FRAZIER, E. FRANKLIN. Black Bourgeoisie. Free Press, 1957. $2.95; paper $.95 (B)
>A challenging book for senior high students who will soon be emerging to seek their places in society. Excellent for contemporary American problems classes in economics.
SH

GINZBERG, ELI. The Negro Potential. Columbia University Press, 1956. Paper $1.45 (B)
>The thesis of this study is that, by not using its full manpower and by ignoring the economic potential of Negroes, the United States suffers an economic loss.
SH

GREGORY, DICK. Nigger! An Autobiography. E. P. Dutton, 1964. $4.95; Pocket Books paper $.75 (LJ)
>This autobiography of a Negro entertainer tells what it is like to grow up as a Negro in America. He includes his part in the Negro protest movement.
SH

GRIFFIN, JOHN HOWARD. Black Like Me. Houghton Mifflin, 1961. $3.50; New American Library paper $.60 (SH)
A white reporter describes his experiences traveling in the Deep South while disguised as a Negro.
SH

HILL, S. E. See Norgren, Paul H., page 87.

ISAACS, HAROLD R. New World of Negro Americans. John Day, 1963. $7.50; Viking paper $1.65 (SH)
This collection of interviews with Negroes traces the impact of world affairs on Negro Americans.
SH

LOGAN, RAYFORD. The Negro in American Life and Thought. Dial Press, 1954. $5.00; later edition, **The Betrayal of the Negro.** Collier, 1965. Paper $1.50 (B)
This book is a study of the political, social, and economic aspects of the "Negro problem" during the last quarter of the nineteenth century.
SH

MALCOLM X. Autobiography. Grove Press, 1965. $7.50; Dell paper $.95 (SH)
The story of Malcolm X as he dictated it to a journalist friend shortly before his assassination in February, 1965.
SH

MURPHY, W. S. See Cohen, Jerry, page 84.

MYRDAL, GUNNAR. An American Dilemma. Harper & Row, 1944. $16.50; McGraw-Hill, 2 vols. 1964. Paper $3.45 each (SH)
This classic study of race relations by the noted Swedish social economist points out the effect of inequality on every phase of the lives and personalities of Negroes.
SH

NORGREN, PAUL H., and HILL, S. E. Toward Fair Employment. Columbia University Press, 1964. $8.50 (LJ)

A general book that surveys the history of fair employment legislation to 1963. The author believes that state and federal laws could do much to bring about fair employment.
SH

NORTHWOOD, L. K., and BARTH, ERNEST A. Urban Desegregation: Negro Pioneers and Their White Neighbors. University of Washington Press, 1965. $3.95

A study made from interviews obtained in fifteen instances of successful integration of Negro families into previously all-white neighborhoods in Seattle, Washington.
SH

OSOFSKY, GILBERT. Harlem: The Making of a Ghetto: Negro New York, 1890–1930. Harper & Row, 1966. $6.95 (C)

An account of the evolution of an aristocratic upper-class white community into a crowded Negro ghetto.
SH

PARKS, GORDON. A Choice of Weapons. Harper & Row, 1966. $5.95; Berkley paper $.75 (LJ)

An internationally known Life photographer, author, and composer tells of his struggles during the Thirties and Forties to overcome the obstacles of poverty and a black skin. His story shows how a talented and determined Negro made dignity, hard work, and love his weapons in the fight against discrimination.
SH

REDDING, J. SAUNDERS. On Being Negro in America. Bobbs-Merrill, 1951. $1.35 (B)

An analysis of the "Negro problem" by one who met it in church, college, and through his own son's experiences with other "American" boys.
SH

ROBINSON, JAMES H. Road Without Turning. Farrar, Straus, 1950. $3.00 (B)

An autobiography of a Negro minister who tells of his struggle to rise to the ministry from a slum in Knoxville, Tennessee.

SH

ROSE, ARNOLD. The Negro in America. Peter Smith, 1956. $4.00; Harper paper $1.95 (SH)

A useful distillation of the important analyses, insights, and conclusions in Myrdal's monumental study, **An American Dilemma.** The paperback price makes it possible to have classroom sets for maximum class participation.

SH

ROSEN, DAVID H. See Rosen, Harry M., page 88.

ROSEN, HARRY M., and ROSEN, DAVID H. But Not Next Door. Ivan Oblensky, 1962. $5.00 (B)

Dramatic account of the Deerfield, Illinois, case in which an interracial housing development was thwarted. Describes the reaction of Deerfield residents when they learned prematurely that some of the housing units were to be sold to Negroes.

SH

ROWAN, CARL. Go South to Sorrow. Random House, 1957. $4.95 (B)

A Negro journalist gives an account of a trip he made to the South in 1956—impressions and interviews with both whites and Negroes.

SH

RUTLAND, EVA. The Trouble with Being a Mama. Abingdon, 1964. $2.95

A Negro mother gives an account of the problems in raising a family of four children, and how they are met. She could be almost any mother.

JH-SH

STRINGFELLOW, WILLIAM. My People Is the Enemy. Holt, Rinehart & Winston, 1964. $3.95; Doubleday paper $.95 (LJ)

An Episcopalian layman and lawyer, who has lived and worked in Harlem, challenges Christians and the ethics that control their acts. The economic and sociological meaning of the ghettos is examined in detail and could be used as the basis for discussion and debate in areas where there is no undue concern regarding the separation of religion and state.

SH

TUSSMAN, JOSEPH (editor). The Supreme Court on Racial Discrimination. Oxford University Press, 1963. Paper $1.95

Comments and excerpts from leading Supreme Court decisions that deal with segregation in education, traveling, and eating places, and with discrimination in jobs, housing, jury duty, and voting.

JH-SH

WEAVER, ROBERT C. Dilemmas of Urban America. Harvard University Press, 1965. $3.50; Atheneum paper $1.95 (LJ)

A source book on new communities, urban renewal, and problems of race in housing development and community growth.

SH

WILLIAMS, JOHN A. This Is My Country, Too. New American Library, 1965. $.60 (NYT)

A Negro writer tours the United States after the passage of the Public Accommodation Law. This book could be used as background material for discussions of law and order as well as of the social customs of the country.

SH

WOODWARD, C. VANN. The Strange Career of Jim Crow. Oxford University Press, 1966. $4.50; paper $1.50

Mr. Woodward has revised the 1955 edition of his book that describes the "on again–off again" patterns of racial segregation from slavery times to the present.

SH

SPORTS

Elementary

ALOU, FELIPE, and WEISKOPF, HERM. Felipe Alou: My Life and Baseball. Word, 1967. $3.95

The story of Alou's life of poverty in the Dominican Republic and his desire to excel in major league baseball.

UE

DUCKETT, ALFRED. See Robinson, Jackie, page 91.

HIRSHBERG, AL. Bill Russell of the Boston Celtics. Julian Messner, 1963. $3.25

An inspirational story of the tall defensive wizard of the basketball courts.

UE

ROBINSON, JACKIE. Baseball Has Done It. J. B. Lippincott, 1964. $3.50 (SH)

Frank Robinson, Hank Aaron, Jim Gilliam, Ernie Banks, and other Negro baseball players tell what it is to be a baseball star and a Negro at the same time.

UE

ROBINSON, JACKIE, and DUCKETT, ALFRED. Break-through to the Big League: The Story of Jackie Robinson. Harper & Row, 1965. $3.50 (ES)

An autobiography of the Negro who broke through the racial barriers in professional baseball. The book is easy to read, has many interesting photographs and will be enjoyed by pupils of a wide range with average or below-average reading ability.

UE

SHAPIRO, MILTON J. The Hank Aaron Story. Julian Messner, 1961. $2.95

A well-presented account of the life of an outstanding baseball hero.

UE

WEISKOPF, HERM. See Alou, Felipe, page 90.

Secondary

ALOU, FELIPE, and WEISKOPF, HERM. Felipe Alou: My Life and Baseball.

See page 90.

BONTEMPS, ARNA. Famous Negro Athletes. Dodd, Mead, 1964. $3.50 (LJ)

A collection of biographies of popular Negro athletes, showing the struggles of each to succeed. Among those included are Joe Louis, Satchel Paige, Jesse Owens, Wilt Chamberlain, and Althea Gibson.

JH-SH

BROWN, JAMES N., and COPE, MYRON. Off My Chest. Doubleday, 1964. $4.95 (B)

An autobiography of the Cleveland Browns' famous fullback, Jimmy Brown.

JH-SH

COPE, MYRON. See Brown, James N., page 91.

GIBSON, ALTHEA. I Always Wanted to be Somebody. Harper & Row, 1959. $4.95 (SH)

Althea Gibson's story of her rise from the streets of Harlem to become a great international tennis player.
JH-SH

HIRSHBERG, AL. Bill Russell of the Boston Celtics.
See page 90.

McSWEENY, W. See Russell, William, page 92.

OLSEN, JACK. Black Is Best. G. P. Putnam, 1968. $4.95 (LJ)

A look at some of the causes of Cassius Clay's angry retreat from a world that wanted so much to like him.
SH

ROBINSON, JACKIE. Baseball Has Done It.
See page 90.

ROBINSON, LOUIE. Arthur Ashe, Tennis Champion. Doubleday, 1967. $2.95

Arthur Ashe is the first male Negro to make the big time in a stronghold of white athletes.
JH-SH

RUSSELL, WILLIAM F., and McSWEENY, W. Go Up for Glory. Coward-McCann, 1966. $5.00 (LJ)

Bill Russell, superstar basketball player, tells of his struggle to achieve success.
JH-SH

SHAPIRO, MILTON J. The Hank Aaron Story.
See page 91.

TUNNELL, EMLEM. Footsteps of a Giant. Doubleday, 1966. $4.95 (LJ)

> Tunnell relates his rise from poverty in Garrett Hill, Pennsylvania, to become a football and basketball star on the Toledo University and Coast Guard teams and a coach and scout for the New York Giants football team.
> **JH-SH**

WEISKOPF, HERM. See Alou, Felipe, page 90.

YOUNG, A. S., "DR." Negro Firsts in Sports. Johnson, 1963 $4.95.

> A popular history of Negroes in American sports from the early boxers in the 1800's to Althea Gibson, "the first Negro woman ever admitted to the U.S. Lawn Tennis Association Championships."
> **JH-SH**

REFERENCE BOOKS

DAVIS, JOHN P. (editor). American Negro Reference Book.
Prentice-Hall, 1965. $22.50 (SH)
A comprehensive reference work that surveys every phase
of the life of Negroes in the United States.
JH-SH

International Library of Negro Life and History. 5 vols. Association for the Study of Negro Life and History, 1967. $60.00
The contents include: Volume I, Anthology of the American Negro in the Theatre; Volume II, History of the Negro
in Medicine; Volume III, Historical Negro Biographies; Volume IV, Negro Americans in the Civil War; Volume V, The
Negro in Music and Art.
JH-SH

The Negro Handbook. Johnson, 1966. $12.50 (C)
The book includes sections on population, vital statis-
tics, civil rights, crime, education, libraries, economy, government and politics, armed forces, sports, religion, the pro-
fessions, farms and farming, creative arts, the press, Negro
monuments, a biographical dictionary, obituaries, and a di-
rectory of Negroes holding elective or appointive positions

in state, municipal, and county agencies and Negro organizations. Will be helpful in making reports and doing research on current questions about Negroes.
SH

PLOSKI, HARRY A., and BROWN, ROSCOE C., JR. Negro Almanac. Bellwether, 1967. $22.00 (LJ)
The Negro Almanac offers ready facts about the Negro in one compact volume. It includes an extensive historical review of major events in Negro history from 1492 to 1954.
JH-SH

SLOAN, IRVIN J. The American Negro: A Chronology and Fact Book. Oceana, 1965. Paper $1.50
Beginning with the arrival of the first African slaves in Lisbon, Portugal (1442), this book lists dates of significant events through the Selma, Alabama, March in 1965. Included are: (1) a selected bibliography on the Negro American; (2) a list of Negro colleges and universities by states; (3) a list of Negro organizations; (4) a list of Negro newspapers and periodicals by states; and (5) the First Civil Rights Act of 1866.
JH-SH

MAGAZINES AND
NEWSPAPERS

Afro-American (Newspaper, weekly). 628 West Utah Street, Baltimore, Maryland.

Chicago Defender (Newspaper, daily). 2400 South Michigan Avenue, Chicago, Illinois.

Ebony Magazine (Monthly). 1820 South Michigan Avenue, Chicago, Illinois.

Freedomways (Magazine, quarterly). Freedomways Associates, Inc. 799 Broadway, New York, New York.

Interracial Review (Magazine, monthly). Catholic Interracial Council of New York. 233 Broadway, New York, New York.

Journal of Negro Education (Magazine, quarterly). Association for the Study of Negro Life and History. 1538 Ninth Street, N.W., Washington, D.C.

Journal of Negro History (Magazine, quarterly). Association for the Study of Negro Life and History. 1538 Ninth Street, N.W., Washington, D.C.

Negro Digest (Magazine, monthly). Johnson Publishing Company. 1820 South Michigan Avenue, Chicago, Illinois.

Negro History Bulletin (Magazine, monthly). Association for the Study of Negro Life and History. 1538 Ninth Street, N.W., Washington, D.C.

New York Amsterdam News (Newspaper, weekly). 2340 Eighth Avenue, New York, New York.

Phylon (Magazine, quarterly). Atlanta University. 223 Chestnut Street, S.W., Atlanta, Georgia.

Pittsburgh Courier (Newspaper, weekly). 2628 Centre Avenue, Pittsburgh, Pennsylvania.

Southern School News (Magazine, monthly). Southern Educational Reporting Service. Box 6156, Acklen Station, Nashville, Tennessee.

Tuesday (Monthly roto supplement in major newspapers). Tuesday Publications. 605 Third Avenue, New York, New York.

AUDIOVISUAL MATERIALS

PHONOGRAPH RECORDS

Adventures in Negro History, Vol. I. Distributed by Pepsi-Cola Bottling Co.

>   Record (HRP-101, L.P.) accompanying filmstrip.

Adventures in Negro History, Vol. II. The Frederick Douglass Years 1817-1895. Distributed by Pepsi-Cola Bottling Co.

>   Record accompanying filmstrip.

Been in the Storm So Long. Recorded by Guy Carawan. Folkways FS 3842. $4.25

>   Spirituals, shouts, game songs from South Carolina Sea Islands.

BENÉT, STEPHEN VINCENT. John Brown's Body. Anti-Defamation League of B'nai B'rith, 43 minutes.

>   Richard Boone and Douglas Campbell are the narrators, accompanied by the CBS Orchestra.

BERKERT, CARL. Freedom Songs: Selma, Alabama. Folkways FH 5594. $5.79
> Descriptive notes of the Selma March in 1965 and texts of the songs sung during the march.

BONTEMPS, ARNA. Anthology of Negro Poets. Folkways FL 9791. $5.79
> Poets reading their own works are: Langston Hughes, Sterling Brown, Claude McKay, Countee Cullen, Margaret Walker, and Gwendolyn Brooks. Biographical notes by Arna Bontemps.

――――. **An Anthology of Negro Poets in the U.S.A.—200 Years.** Folkways FP 9792. $5.79
> Read by poet Arna Bontemps. Selected from American Negro poets of past 200 years; includes ex-slave Phillis Wheatley, Paul Laurence Dunbar, Countee Cullen, and others.

――――. **Negro Poetry for Young People.** Folkways FC 7114. $4.25
> Readings of poetry by Paul Laurence Dunbar, Beatrice Murphy, Claude McKay, and Helen Johnson.

BROWN, STERLING, and HUGHES, LANGSTON. Sterling Brown and Langston Hughes Read Their Poems. Folkways FP 9790. $5.79

DAVIS, OSSIE. The Autobiography of Frederick Douglass. Folkways FH 5522. $5.79
> Readings based on the autobiographical works of Douglass.

DAWSON, WILLIAM L. Negro Folk Symphony. Decca DL 10077. $4.79
> A symphonic work based on folk themes by William Dawson. The orchestra is conducted by Leopold Stokowski.

DUBERMAN, MARTIN B. In White America. Columbia KOL-6030. $5.79
> Documentary history of Negroes in the United States.

DUBOIS, W. E. B. Interviewed by Moses Asch. Folkways FH 5511. $5.79
    A recorded autobiography that tells of the NAACP, the **Crisis** magazine, Africa, the Negro, and young people.

GRAHAM, GORDON, and WILLIAMS, HUGH. Great Moments in Negro History, Vol. I. AG 303. $1.49
    Words and music combine to unveil the little-known heritage of the American Negro.

HUGHES, LANGSTON. The Best of Simple. Read by Melvin Stewart. Folkways FL 9789. $5.79
    Selected stories of Jessie B. Simple.
————. **The Dream Keeper.** Folkways F 7104. $4.15
    Langston Hughes's poems for children. A text is included with the record.
————. **First Album of Jazz for Children.** Folkways FP 712. $4.25
    Begins with music in Africa and progresses to New Orleans jazz and its later development. Included is the music of Jelly Roll Morton, Bunk Johnson, Duke Ellington, and Ma Rainey.
————. **The Glory of Negro History.** Folkways FC 7752. $5.79
    Written and narrated by Langston Hughes. Negroes in America from earliest times to the present.
————. **Jericho–Jim Crow.** Folkways 9671. $11.58
    Play with incidental music performed by the Hugh Porter Gospel Singers, with piano, organ, and percussion. Biographical notes and text of the play included.
————. **Tambourines to Glory.** Folkways FG 3538. $5.79
    Gospel songs by Hughes recorded at Second Canaan Baptist Church in New York City.
————. See Brown, Sterling, page 99.

JENKINS, ELLA. American Negro Folk and Work Song Rhythms. Folkways FC 7654. $5.79
    Ella Jenkins and the Goodwill Spiritual Choir use per-

cussion instruments and hand clapping. Includes "No More Auction Block," "You Better Mind," "This Is the Way I Pray."

JOHNSON, JAMES WELDON. God's Trombones. Folkways FL 9788. $5.79

Poems, read by Bryce Bond, with background music for piano by William Martin.

KENNEDY, JOHN F. John F. Kennedy and the Negro. Johnson Publishing Company, XCTV-96558. $2.00

Civil rights statements from Kennedy's great speeches.

LARUE, MICHAEL. American Negro Songs from Slavery Times. Folkways 5252. $4.25

Michael Larue sings slave songs accompanied by guitar. Included are informative notes by John Hope Franklin and words to each song.

LEDBETTER, HUDDIE. Negro Folk Songs for Young People. Folkways FD 7533. $5.79

The noted folk singer sings and narrates "John Henry," "Good Morning," "Blues," "Rock Island Line," "We're In the Same Boat," and four spirituals.

————. **Leadbelly . . . Last Sessions.** Folkways FA 2941 A/B Vol. 1, Part 1; FA 2941 C/D Vol. 1, Part 2; FA 2942 A/B Vol. 2, Part 1; FA 2942 C/D Vol. 2, Part 2. $11.58

On these records, you will hear Leadbelly the singer and Leadbelly the man. Folk music lovers, blues fans, scholars— all have turned to this unique document as the basic source for knowledge and appreciation of the genius of Leadbelly. Ninety-four different songs are performed in this set.

MONTGOMERY GOSPEL TRIO and the NASHVILLE QUARTET. We Shall Overcome. Folkways FH 5591. $5.79

Songs of the Freedom Riders and the Sit-Ins. Spirituals, gospels, and new songs performed by student groups and folk singers. Booklet of song texts included.

NASHVILLE QUARTET. See Montgomery Gospel Trio, page 101.

O'NEAL, FREDERICK, and SIMMS, HILDA. 1, 2, 3, & A **Zing Zing Zing.** Folkways FC 7003. $4.15
> Street games and songs of the children of New York City, such as skip rope chants, ball-bouncing games, and camp songs.

The Sit-In Story. Documentary with voices of Rev. Martin Luther King, Jr., Rev. Ralph Abernathy. Folkways FH 5502. $5.79
> Story of the lunchroom sit-ins, presented by Friendly World Broadcasting, Edwin Randall, narrator. Includes voices of Ralph McGill and Peggy Alexander.
> **SH**

SIMMS, HILDA. See O'Neal, Frederick, page 102.

WASHINGTON, DOROTHY. The **Negro Woman.** Folkways FH 5523. $5.79
> Quotations from the speeches or writings of seven Negro women, beginning with a poem by Phillis Wheatley and including selections from Sojourner Truth, Harriet Tubman, Frances Ellen Watkins Harper, Ida B. Wells Barnett, Mary Church Terrell, and Mary McLeod Bethune. A long bibliography is included.
> **SH**

WILLIAMS, HUGH. See Graham, Gordon, page 100.

FILMS AND FILMSTRIPS

Adventures in Negro History, Vol. I. Distributed by the Pepsi-Cola Bottling Co. Free.

Filmstrip (65 frames) includes many Negroes who were important in the development of America.

Recording accompanies filmstrip.

JH-SH

Adventures in Negro History, Vol. II. The Frederick Douglass Years, 1817-1895. Distributed by the Pepsi-Cola Bottling Co. Free.

Recording accompanies filmstrip.

JH-SH

Booker T. Washington. EBF. 18 minutes. B & W. $3.90

Tells the dramatic story of Booker T. Washington from childhood to the time when he became "probably the greatest Negro in history."

UE-JH-SH

Epitaph for Jim Crow. Anti-Defamation League of B'nai B'rith. 4 films.

A series of fine illustrated film-lectures on the dynamics of intergroup relations in the United States, including the history and current situation of the Negro American. The film reviews the historical, political, sociological, and psychological forces that shape patterns of prejudice and discrimination, and touches on new advances in intergroup relations. Produced in cooperation with the National Educational Television Network and Harvard University. Dr. Thomas Pettigrew of the Harvard faculty is the host-narrator.

"Face to Face" explores the problems of bringing diverse groups together and the value of various kinds of contact.

"A Tale of Two Ladies" is a review of the history of Negro protest against racial discrimination.

"The Newest New Negro" explores the meaning and value of the newest forms of direct-action protest against segregation. Whitney Young, Director of the National Urban League, is narrator.

"Conformity and the Crutch" discusses the psychology of bigotry and the differences between pathological bigotry and bigotry arising out of social conformity in the light of recent sociological research.

JH-SH

Face of the South. Anti-Defamation League of B'nai B'rith. 30 minutes. Color cleared for TV.

Historical analysis of economic and social factors that have made the South what it is today. An illustrated lecture by George Mitchell, former Director of the Southern Regional Council.

SH

Felicia. University of California. 13 minutes. $75.00. Rental $5.00.

Felicia, a fifteen-year-old Negro girl, tells the story of life in Watts prior to the riots of 1965.

JH-SH

For All My Students. University of California. 36 minutes. Rental $10.00

"The particular problems and rewards of teaching Negro high school students are dramatically revealed in this film, which contrasts poor and effective teaching in integrated classroom situations and follows several students' histories."

SH

For White Christians Only. Anti-Defamation League of B'nai B'rith. 30 minutes. B & W. Rental only. $5.00

A kinescope of the NBC-National Educational Television program on housing discrimination against minorities—specifically, Negroes and Jews. In addition to a round table discussion with three experts, Jackie Robinson describes his house-hunting experiences, and a Fairfield County, Connecticut, real estate broker shows how housing discrimination against Jews operates in his area.
SH

Free at Last. Indiana University. 30 minutes. B & W. CS-1665. $125.00. Rental $5.40
Dramatic readings from the works of Frederick Douglass, Booker T. Washington, W. E. B. DuBois, and Marcus Garvey are featured.
SH

Future and the Negro. Indiana University. 75 minutes. B & W. CS-1669. Rental $10.90
Presents a panel discussion on the subject of the Negro's future.
SH

Harriet Tubman and the Underground Railroad. McGraw-Hill. 54 minutes. B & W. $10.75
Portrays the conflicts and trials involved in a slave's flight to freedom.
SH

Heritage of the Negro. Indiana University. 30 minutes. B & W. CS-1661. Rental $5.40
Emphasizes that African history as recorded by white historians has traditionally ignored the old civilizations of Africa below the Sahara. Explores the art, sculpture, and present-day pageantry which reflect the old cultures.
SH

History of the Negro in America. Text-Film Division, McGraw-Hill. 3 films. 20 minutes each. B & W. $4.55 each.

Film series traces the historical background of the struggle to fulfill the promise of American democracy—the realization of freedom and equality for all. Using carefully selected graphic materials, photographs, and newsreel footage, this series accurately portrays the entire span of the vital role of Negroes in American history. These films will be a fresh and stimulating supplement to classes in American history.

"Out of Slavery, 1619-1860." This film traces the history of the American ideal of equal rights for all—a promise kept by some, but misinterpreted and even broken by others. After a dramatic prologue—the proclamation of the Declaration of Independence—students examine some of the steps that led to the Civil War. They view slavery as it was practiced in ancient Greece and Rome, and civilization as it existed in West Africa on the eve of the slave trade. They witness the uprooting of millions of Negroes from Africa and their passage into bondage in the New World. And, most importantly, they experience the life of Negroes in the North and in the South as freemen and as slaves, as patriots during the American Revolution, and as participants in the abolitionist movement.

"Civil War and Reconstruction, 1861-1877." This film dramatizes two critical periods in history that have had a profound effect upon the development of American life. Students begin to understand why political conflict over slavery was the root cause of the Civil War, what Negroes did to help win their own freedom in that war, why Lincoln issued the Emancipation Proclamation, and the problem of reconstructing the nation when the war was over. Viewers witness the brief but exciting period of reform—the reconstruction that followed the war. Not only will this film stimulate students to trace the causes and effects of this period, but it will also show them how the Emancipation Proclamation and the Thirteenth, Fourteenth, and Fifteenth

Amendments sought to protect and preserve the newly-won freedom of Negroes.

"Freedom Movement, 1877-Today." In this film, the students see Negroes abandoned by the North, shut out of political life in the South, still suffering under jim crowism, forced into a sharecropper-tenant farm life or penned up in the black ghettos of the big cities. They begin to understand the complex chain of events that fostered these developments and to see how they might have been prevented. They can sense the fresh and invigorating spirit of the cultural renaissance of the New Negro of the 1920's. Finally, they see why the period since 1950 has kindled renewed support for an active civil rights program.
JH-SH

Leading American Negroes. Visual Society of Education, Chicago, Illinois. $39.75

Each filmstrip portrays the life of an outstanding man or woman whose contribution to American life is a part of our national heritage. Popular with both young people and adults, the filmstrips average fourteen minutes each, running time. The people included in the set are:

Mary McLeod Bethune (48 frames) George Washington Carver (45 frames)	with 2 guides, 1 record $15.00
Benjamin Banneker (44 frames) Robert Smalls (43 frames)	with 2 guides, 1 record $15.00
Frederick Douglass (45 frames) Harriet Tubman (45 frames)	with 2 guides, 1 record $15.00

UE-JH-SH

Negro and the American Promise. Indiana University. 60 minutes. B & W. NET-2500. Rental $8.15

Presents Dr. Kenneth Clark, Professor of Psychology at the City College of New York, interviewing James Baldwin

and Martin Luther King, Jr., campaigning for integration and non-discrimination, and Malcolm X, whose extreme position calls for a special segregation from the "whites."
JH-SH

Negro and the South. Indiana University. 30 minutes. B & W. CS-1662. Rental $5.40

Interviews both Negroes and whites of Mississippi to depict "the Southern way of life." White persons interviewed include a mayor, a sheriff, and a judge. Negroes interviewed include a teacher, a mechanic, and a minister.
JH-SH

Negro Heroes from American History. A John Simons Film. 11 minutes. $125.00

An introduction to the history of the Negro in America through the biography of several heroes, from the Revolutionary War to the present day.
JH-SH

New Horizons in Vocations. Dibie-Dash Productions (4949 Hollywood Blvd., Suite 217, Hollywood, California 90027). 20 minutes. Color. $200.00

The film offers four vignettes on the lives and vocations of people from several ethnic groups, then visits nine other persons in their job environments; it points out the importance of choosing an occupation intelligently. Similar to **They Beat the Odds,** by the same producer. The technical production is excellent and the film should make a strong impression on minority-group youths planning their futures.
JH-SH

New Mood. Indiana University. 30 minutes. B & W. CS-1667. Rental $5.40

Reviews the civil rights struggle of the past decade and traces the impact of the new Negro militancy on both white and Negro Americans.
JH-SH

Omowale—The Child Returns Home. Indiana University. 30 minutes. B & W. CS-1666. Rental $5.40

John Williams, Mississippi-born Negro, explores his ancestral roots. He explores the relationship of the American Negro to the Africans and Africa.

JH-SH

Our Country, Too. Indiana University. 30 minutes. B & W. CS-1668. Rental $5.40

Explores the inner world of the American Negro—his values, attitudes, and impressions of life. Interviews at various places, including an African rite in Harlem, a Negro debutante ball, the office of a Negro newspaper, and a Negro-owned radio station, help to depict the Negro's view of the world.

SH

They Beat the Odds. Dibie-Dash Productions. (4949 Hollywood Blvd., Suite 217, Hollywood, California 90027). 22 minutes. Color. $220.00

A Negro boy considers dropping out of school. In a conference with his counselor he admits his feeling that Negroes have too many odds against them, but his mind is changed as the counselor tells him of several Negroes who have become successful in widely varied fields, such as fashion design, education, business, egg production, space, chemistry, etc. The quality of photography and sound is excellent, and the color adds greatly to the impact. Excellent for guidance as well as general information on current job status of Negroes.

JH-SH

Walk in My Shoes. McGraw-Hill. 54 minutes. B & W. $10.65

The film explores the world of the Negro and listens to him as he speaks in many voices. He speaks for and against the Black Muslims, Martin Luther King, Jr., Freedom Riders, integration, and the NAACP.

SH

Where Is Jim Crow? A Conversation with Brock Peters. University of California. 30 minutes. Rental $10.00

> Brock Peters discusses the difficulties facing the Negro actor in Hollywood and intimates that the film capitol of the world has one Negro star and is not willing to have another.
> **SH**

Where Is Jim Crow? A Conversation with Nancy Wilson. University of California. 30 minutes. Rental $10.00

> "Would Nancy Wilson, secretary, be accepted as Nancy Wilson, singer, is?" This is a question Miss Wilson poses and attempts to answer as she discusses civil rights and the Negro in show business.
> **SH**

Where is Jim Crow? A Conversation with Stokely Carmichael. University of California. 30 minutes. Rental $10.00

> The controversial former National Chairman of the Student Non-Violent Coordinating Committee and spokesman for the concept of "Black Power" describes the police attack upon civil rights demonstrators in Montgomery, Alabama, in 1965, and discusses the aims of the "Freedom Movement."
> **SH**

PICTURES

ASSOCIATION FOR THE STUDY OF NEGRO LIFE AND HISTORY. Outstanding Negroes.

> Pictures in assorted sizes and prices. Also lesson plans and other classroom aids.

JOHNSON PUBLISHING COMPANY. Assorted Pictures of Outstanding Negroes.

Children at play, high school students at work, etc.

AFRO-AMERICAN PUBLISHING COMPANY, INC. The Negro in our History.

Twenty-four display prints of great Negroes past and present. A visual education companion to the book of the same name.

CULTURAL EXCHANGE CENTER. Prints by American Negro Artists.

Prints by contemporary Negro artists. The text in the book consists only of the foreword and introduction.

●

APPENDIX I

LIST OF BIOGRAPHIES

●

INDIVIDUAL

Hirshberg, Al. **Bill Russell of the Boston Celtics.** 90, 92

Holt, Rackham. **George Washington Carver: An American Biography.** 42

Hoyt, Edwin Palmer. **Paul Robeson: The American Othello.** 28

Hughes, Langston. **The Big Sea.** (Autobiography) 32

————. **I Wonder as I Wander.** (Autobiography) 32

Jackson, Mahalia, and Wylie, E. M. **Movin' On Up.** (Autobiography) 29

Johnson, James Weldon. **Along This Way.** (Autobiography) 32

Kirkeby, Edward. **Ain't Misbehavin': The Story of Fats Waller.** 29

Kugelmass, Alvin. **Ralph Bunche: Fighter for Freedom.** 78

Kunstler, William M. **Deep in my Heart.** (Autobiography) 49

Malcolm X. **Autobiography.** 86

Manber, David. **Wizard of Tuskegee.** (George Washington Carver) 41

Meltzer, Milton. **Thaddeus Stevens and the Fight for Negro Rights.** 50

Meredith, James. **Three Years in Mississippi.** (Autobiography) 51

Millender, Dharathula. **Crispus Attucks: Boy of Valor.** 14

Miller, Floyd. **Ahdoolo!** (Matthew Henson) 42

Morrow, E. Frederic. **Black Man in the White House.** (Autobiography) 78

Nathan, Hans. **Dan Emmett and the Rise of Early Minstrelsy.** 30

Newman, Shirlee. **Marian Anderson: Lady from Philadelphia.** 30

Olsen, Jack. **Black Is Best.** (Cassius Clay) 92

Parks, Gordon. **A Choice of Weapons.** (Autobiography) 87

Patterson, Lillie. **Booker T. Washington: Leader of His People.** 57

————. **Frederick Douglass: Freedom Fighter.** 62

Pauli, Hertha. **Her Name was Sojourner Truth.** 73

Petry, Ann. **Harriet Tubman: Conductor on the Underground Railroad.** 73

COLLECTED

Bardolph, Richard. **The Negro Vanguard.** 64

Bontemps, Arna. **One Hundred Years of Negro Freedom.** 65

———. **Famous Negro Athletes.** 91

Botkin, B. A. **Lay My Burden Down.** 66

Buckmaster, Henrietta. **Flight to Freedom.** 66

Charters, Samuel Barclay. **The Bluesmen: The Story and the Music of the Men Who Made the Blues.** 27

Commager, Henry Steele. **Crusaders for Freedom.** 66

Cuney-Hare, Maud. **Negro Musicians and their Music.** 27

Dobler, Lavinia, and Toppin, E. A. **Pioneers and Patriots: The Lives of Six Negroes of the Revolutionary Era.** 67

Foley, Albert S. **God's Men of Color.** 39

Hughes, Langston. **Famous American Negroes.** 61, 70

———. **Famous Negro Heroes of America.** 61

———. **Famous Negro Music Makers.** 26, 28

———. **First Book of Jazz.** 28

Johnston, Johanna. **Special Bravery.** 70

Lee, Irvin H. **Negro Medal of Honor Men.** 71

Meltzer, Milton. **In Their Own Words: A History of the American Negro.** 72

Redding, J. Saunders. **The Lonesome Road.** 74

Robinson, Jackie. **Baseball Has Done It.** 90, 92

Rollins, Charlemae H. **Famous American Negro Poets.** 32

———. **Famous Negro Entertainers.** 27, 30

———. **They Showed the Way.** 75

Sterling, Dorothy, and Quarles, Benjamin. **Lift Every Voice.** 76

Sterling, Philip, and Logan, Rayford. **Four Took Freedom.** 76

Sterne, Emma G. **Blood Brothers: Four Men of Science.** 41

———. **I Have a Dream.** 54

———. **They Took Their Stand.** 76

Stratton, Madeline Robinson. **Negroes Who Helped Build America.** 63

Terkel, Studs. **Giants of Jazz.** 30

Young, A. S. **Negro Firsts in Sports.** 93

Young, Margaret B. **First Book of Negroes.** 64

APPENDIX II

SOURCES USED IN
SELECTING MATERIALS

●

A. L. A. Catalog, 1942–1949. Chicago, Illinois: American Library Association.

Basic Book Collection for High Schools. 7th ed. Chicago, Illinois: American Library Association, 1963.

Bibliographic Survey: The Negro in Print, 1965. Washington, D. C.: Negro Bibliographic and Research Center.

Book Review Digest. Bronx, New York: H. W. Wilson Co.

Booklist and Subscription Books Bulletin: A Guide to Current Books, Chicago, Illinois: American Library Association.

Books About Negro Life for Children. Augusta Baker. New York, New York: The New York Public Library.

Books in Print. Index to Publishers' Trade List Annual. New York, New York: R. R. Bowker Company.

Children's Catalog. New York, New York: H. W. Wilson Company, 1963 and supplements.

Doors to More Mature Reading: Detailed Notes on Adult Books for Use with Young People. Chicago, Illinois: American Library Association, 1964.

Ebony. Chicago, Illinois: Johnson Publishing Company, Inc.

Fiction Catalog. 7th ed. New York, New York: H. W. Wilson Company.

Library Journal. New York, New York: R. R. Bowker Company.

Negro Digest. Chicago, Illinois: Johnson Publishing Company.

Negro in the United States. Erwin K. Welsch. Bloomington, Indiana: Indiana University Press, 1965.

Negro History Bulletin. Washington, D. C.: Association for the Study of Negro Life and History.

Negro in America. Elizabeth Miller. Cambridge, Massachusetts: Harvard University Press, 1966.

Negro Life: A Selected Booklist. Mount Vernon, New York: Westchester Library System.

The New York Times Book Review. New York, New York: New York *Times* Company.

School Libraries. Chicago, Illinois: American Library Association.

Subject Guide to Books in Print. New York, New York: R. R. Bowker Company.

Top of the News. Chicago, Illinois: American Library Association.

TITLE AND SUBJECT INDEX

121

AUTHOR INDEX